LOCOMOTIVE PORTFOLIOS

GREAT WESTERN

SMALL-WHEELED DOUBLE-FRAMED 4-4-0 TENDER LOCOMOTIVES

GREAT WESTERN

SMALL-WHEELED DOUBLE-FRAMED 4-4-0 TENDER LOCOMOTIVES

DUKE, BULLDOG, DUKEDOG AND '3521' CLASSES

by

DAVID MAIDMENT

PEN & SWORD
TRANSPORT

First published in Great Britain in 2017 by
Pen & Sword Transport

An imprint of Pen & Sword Books Ltd
47 Church Street, Barnsley, South Yorkshire S70 2AS

ISBN 978 1 47389 645 1

Pen & Sword Books Ltd incorporates the imprints of Pen & Sword
Archaeology, Atlas, Aviation, Battleground, Discovery, Family History,
History, Maritime, Military, Naval, Politics, Railways, Select, Social History,
Transport, True Crime, and Claymore Press, Frontline Books, Leo Cooper,
Praetorian Press, Remember When, Seaforth Publishing and Wharncliffe.

For a complete list of Pen & Sword titles please contact
Pen & Sword Books Limited
47 Church Street, Barnsley, South Yorkshire S70 2AS England
E-mail: enquiries@pen-and-sword.co.uk
Website: www.pen-and-sword.co.uk

Design and typesetting
by Juliet Arthur, www.stimula.co.uk

Printed and bound in China by Imago Publishing Ltd

All David Maidment's royalties from this book will be donated to the
Railway Children charity [reg. no. 1058991] [www.railwaychildren.org.uk]

CONTENTS

Other books by David Maidment:
Novels (Religious historical fiction)
The Child Madonna, Melrose Books, 2009
The Missing Madonna, PublishNation, 2012
The Madonna and Her Sons, PublishNation, 2015

Novels (Railway fiction)
Lives on the Line, Max Books, 2013

Non-fiction (Railways)
The Toss of a Coin, PublishNation, 2014
A Privileged Journey, Pen and Sword, 2015
An Indian Summer of Steam, Pen and Sword, 2015
Great Western Eight-Coupled Heavy Freight Locomotives, Pen and Sword, 2015
Great Western Moguls and Prairies, Pen and Sword, 2016
The Urie and Maunsell 2-cylinder 4-6-0s, Pen and Sword, 2016

Non-fiction (Street Children)
The Other Railway Children, PublishNation, 2012
Nobody ever listened to me, PublishNation, 2012

PREFACE

This volume is one of a series of Pen & Sword books that are portfolios of British steam locomotives – this one about the design, construction and operation of the Great Western smaller wheeled double-framed 4-4-0 locomotives that were designed for the heavily graded lines in Devon and Cornwall. The book has been written by former senior railway manager, David Maidment, with assistance and considerable input from Great Western Trust Photo Archivist, Laurence Waters, drawing on research published by the Railway Correspondence & Travel Society Part 7 of their history of locomotives of the GWR and the David & Charles books on GW standard gauge 4-4-0s published in 1977 and 1978.

I owe grateful thanks to many who have supplied photographs and allowed them to be published free of charge or at much reduced rates as my royalties are being donated to the 'Railway Children' (www.railwaychildren.org.uk), a charity for street and runaway children in India, East Africa and the UK, which I founded in 1995 and is significantly supported by both the UK commercial and heritage railway companies and their suppliers. Thanks are due in particular to the Great Western Trust (Didcot), the Manchester Locomotive Society (Stockport), Mike Bentley and John Hodge, whose collection and knowledge of railway photographs and research in South Wales is unparalleled, and to the Railway Performance Society for permission to quote a few of the train logs in their possession.

This book covers the 5' 8" coupled-wheel 4-4-0s of the 'Duke', 'Bulldog' and 'Earl' ('Dukedog') classes, which first came into existence on the GWR in 1895 and whose final examples just reached the year 1960, and the small group of 5' 2" wheeled 4-4-0s rebuilt at the start of the twentieth century from old broad and standard gauge 0-4-4 saddle and side tank engines. Just one example of this band of four classes of double-framed mixed traffic engines of the 275 built has been preserved, appearing either in its original intended guise as 3217 *Earl of Berkeley* or its later BR livery as 'Dukedog' 9017 based at the Bluebell Railway at Sheffield Park in Sussex. Pen & Sword has commissioned a follow-up book on the larger wheeled (6' 8") express passenger double-framed 4-4-0s – the 'Badmintons', 'Atbaras', 'Flowers' and 'Cities' 4-4-0s.

I would also like to express my thanks to John Scott-Morgan and other staff at Pen & Sword who have been so helpful in the preparation, design, printing and distribution of the book.

David Maidment
July 2016

INTRODUCTION

'Armstrong' class 7' 1"
coupled-wheel 4-4-0
No. 7 *Charles Saunders*
(later renamed
Armstrong), c1900.
(MLS Collection)

In 1892, the Great Western Railway parted finally from its unique seven foot broad gauge, the last conversion in the West of England taking place in May of that year. The first track rebuilding to standard gauge took place in the 1860s and locomotives for both broad and standard gauges were being produced simultaneously by the GWR engineering works at Swindon and Wolverhampton. William Dean succeeded Joseph Armstrong as Chief Locomotive, Carriage and Wagon Superintendent at Swindon in 1877, whilst George Armstrong was in charge of the construction of standard gauge locomotives at the Stafford Road Wolverhampton Works until 1892. Dean's most significant design was the versatile standard gauge 0-6-0 '2301' class, known as the 'Dean Goods', first produced in 1883. With the steady retraction of broad gauge, little development of design for that gauge took place other than preparation for conversion of the more modern locomotives to standard gauge when the axe finally fell.

Dean developed the classic standard gauge 4-2-2 successful express passenger engines in 1894 rebuilding 2-2-2 3021 and its sisters and constructing new from 3031. Then, still in 1894, Dean nominally rebuilt four earlier 2-4-0s, three ex-broad gauge and one standard gauge, as 4-4-0s with 7' 1" coupled wheels, numbered 7, 8, 14 and 16, his first four-coupled engines.

But the GWR urgently needed replacement engines for the heavily graded mainline into Devon and Cornwall for the newly converted standard gauge line. The need was recognised in 1891 and the specification for a suitable design was established in 1893 and in 1895, the first 'Duke' class 4-4-0 with 5' 7½" coupled wheels emerged, 3252 *Duke of Cornwall.*

Construction of forty of these engines (3252 – 3291) took place between 1895 and 1897 and a second batch of 'Dukes' (3312-3331) was built in 1898 and 1899.

One, 3312 named *Bulldog,* appeared with a new experimental boiler which became the prototype for the Swindon Standard No.2

Works photograph of the new 5' 8" couple-wheeled 4-4-0, 3252 *Duke of Cornwall*, 1895. (GW Trust)

boiler and showed the influence of Dean's assistant, George Jackson Churchward, who had been assuming additional responsibilities as Dean's health failed.

Dean's express and secondary four-coupled locomotives continued to be double-framed, requiring precise engineering expertise in Swindon's erecting shop and eventually the GWR had a larger fleet of double-framed engines than any other railway company – only the Dutch and Egyptian railways built such engines in any significant numbers. By the late 1890s, Churchward was taking more and

1898 built 'Duke' 3317 *Jersey* (with straight nameplate on the firebox as built), c1900. (GW Trust)

3312 *Bulldog*, as initially constructed as a 'Duke' with new experimental Churchward designed boiler in 1898, before rebuilding with a Swindon Standard No.2 boiler in 1906, at Swindon, c1900.
(Bob Miller Collection/MLS)

3310 *Waterford*, a 6' 8" coupled wheel 'Badminton' class with the experimental boiler that influenced the design of boilers for the 'Bulldog' and other Churchward 4-4-0 classes.
(Bob Miller Collection/MLS)

more decisions on the design of Dean's fleet of locomotives, whilst increasing his knowledge of foreign (especially French and American) practice and preparing his own plans for his standard designs that would follow in the early 1900s. Dean had by this time also constructed some express passenger 4-4-0s with 6' 8½" coupled wheels, the 'Badminton' class, and in 1897 3310 *Waterford* was equipped with a Churchward boiler, so that both the 5' 7½" and 6' 8½" variants had boilers that became the pattern for 4-4-0s to be constructed during Churchward's term of office.

In October 1899, 5' 7½ wheeled 3352 *Camel* appeared with a domeless coned boiler, building on the experience with 3310 and 3312 and became the true prototype of the 'Bulldog' class which eventually numbered 156 locomotives, the remainder built between 1900 and 1910 (the last 'lot', named after birds only being completed in January 1910).

The locomotive numbers filled in the blank 3332–3351 space and then ran from 3353-3472 inclusive and 370–3745. Twenty 'Dukes' were rebuilt with Standard No.2 boilers between 1902 and 1909 and thus in effect became 'Bulldogs', forty being retained as 'Dukes' with their smaller original boilers to retain their 'yellow' route classification which

was important for the performance of some of their duties.

Finally, between 1899 and 1902 Churchward set about rebuilding forty Dean 0-4-4Ts, 3521–3560, as useful mixed traffic 4-4-0s with

5' 2" coupled wheels and Belpaire firebox. These engines had an interesting history as they had started life as broad and standard gauge 0-4-2 and 0-4-4 tank engines in the West Country before the final

The prototype 'Camel' class (later 'Bulldog') as built in 1899, 3352 *Camel*. (GW Trust)

3306 *Armorel* the first 'Duke' (formerly numbered 3273) to be rebuilt as a 'Bulldog' with the Standard No.2 boiler in 1902. (Bob Miller Collection/MLS)

Rebuilt '3521' 0-4-4T class, 3553 rebuilt as a 5' 2" couple-wheeled 4-4-0 by Churchward.
(Bob Miller Collection/MLS)

'Duke' 3254 *Cornubia* as renumbered post 1912, formerly 3255. 3253 had been rebuilt as a 'Bulldog' and renumbered as 3300, so the 'Duke' numbers closed up to remove the gaps produced by the rebuildings.
(MLS Collection)

track conversion to standard gauge in May 1892.

One might express surprise that Churchward continued to design and construct traditional GW double-framed 4-4-0s in the first decade of the twentieth century, but the railway clearly needed a safe interim group of relatively modern locomotives while Churchward was developing his more revolutionary standard designs, which initially covered express passenger and heavy freight work as priorities. Churchward did not design the mixed traffic 2-6-0 43XX locomotives until 1911, which then superseded

the small-wheeled 4-4-0s making the further construction of 'Bulldogs' unnecessary. Churchward's policy was to test his new prototype designs thoroughly before commencing full production, so it was 1906-7 before express passenger motive power (the 2900 'Saints') rendered the further construction of 6' 8½ " 4-4-0s redundant.

In 1912, the GWR embarked on a complete renumbering of its locomotive fleet which has created some confusion over the years as the new numbers of the 'Dukes' and 'Bulldogs' were very similar to the old. The 'Dukes' 3252–3291 became

3252–3280, removing the numbers of the 'Dukes' rebuilt as 'Bulldogs' which became 3300–3310, and rebuilds in the 3312–3331 series became 3311–3319. Just to add to the confusion, eleven of the 3312-3331 'Dukes' were not rebuilt, so they were renumbered 3281–3291. The 'Bulldogs' numbered from 3300 (the first twenty being the rebuilt 'Dukes') and continued right through from 3320 to 3455 without any gaps.

By the 1930s, both 'Bulldogs' and 'Dukes' were being withdrawn as the number of mixed traffic 'Halls' were added to the 43XX moguls,

Rebuilt 'Duke' 3309 *Maristow*, formerly 3282, numbered in the 'Bulldog' 3300 series after 1912, seen here at Wellington (Shropshire). (Alan Gilbert Collection/MLS)

3265 *Tre Pol and Pen* rebuilt with the frames of 'Bulldog' 3365 *Charles Grey Mott*, as the prototype 'Dukedog' in 1929, here seen at Banbury, 29 January 1939.
(W. Potter/MLS Collection)

3204 *Earl of Dartmouth*, rebuilt in August 1936 using the frames of 'Bulldog' 3439 and the boiler, cab and motion from 'Duke' 3271 *Eddystone*, seen here at Wolverhampton Stafford Road depot, c1937.
(W.H. Whitworth/MLS Collection)

now numbering in the hundreds. However, the former Cambrian lines around Machynlleth, Barmouth, and Portmadoc were severely restricted on civil engineering grounds and could only take 'yellow' route availability engines, that is the Cambrian engines, the 'Dean Goods' and 'Dukes' but not the 'Bulldogs', whose axle-weights were too heavy. The 'Duke' frames were getting worn by this time and much patched and in January 1930, 'Bulldog' 3365 *Charles Grey Mott* was withdrawn at the same time as 'Duke' 3265 *Tre Pol and Pen* whose frames were life

expired. Apparently 3365's frames were in good condition so the boiler of one was matched with the frames of the other to extend the life of 'yellow' route engines for the former Cambrian routes. The resultant hybrid engine retained its 'Duke' number and name although normally an engine's identity was linked to its frame.

With more pressure on finding suitable engines for the Cambrian section as older engines were withdrawn, a decision was made to replicate this hybrid, with 'Duke' boilers being fitted to withdrawn 'Bulldog' frames, creating what was initially known as the 'Earl' class, numbered 3200–3219, subsequently nicknamed the 'Dukedogs' when their names were removed for attachment to the latest 'Castles'. This rebuilding took place between 1936 and 1938, with an initial twenty and there were plans to similarly rebuild the other twenty 'Dukes' but only 3220-3228 had been completed before war intervened in 1939.

Further renumbering took place in 1946 as the 3200-3700 numbers were required as more Collett and Hawksworth standard locomotives were built, both before and after nationalisation, and the few remaining 'Dukes' and all the 'Dukedogs' were renumbered in the

'Duke' 9076, originally 3287 *St Agnes*, renumbered 3276 in 1912, seen here at Shrewsbury depot on 21 June 1947.
(MLS Collection)

The last 'Dukedog' in service, 9017, here seen earlier leaving Machynlleth with a stopping train to Moat Lane, later preserved on the Bluebell Railway, 20 August 1951.

(N. Fields/MLS Collection)

90XX series, retaining their last two digits, so 3200-3228, became 9000–9028 and 3264 became 9064 etc.

The few remaining 'Dukes' were withdrawn between 1949 and 1951 (the last survivor was 9089, the erstwhile 3326 *St Austell*, later 3289

and unnamed), the last 'Bulldogs' were a pair of the 'Bird' series, Reading-based 3453 *Seagull* and 3454 *Skylark*, withdrawn in November 1951. The 'Dukedogs' retained their mid-Wales work from Machynlleth and Oswestry depots until the late 1950s, with 9014 and 9017 not condemned until October 1960. 9017, the former 3217 allocated the name *Earl of Berkeley*, was preserved based at the Bluebell Railway, and with the 6' 8"

wheeled 3440 *City of Truro*, are the only two double-framed GWR 4-4-0s in existence.

This book will describe in greater detail the design, construction and operation of the three main 5' 7½" wheeled 4-4-0 classes and the '3521' class rebuilds of the earlier Dean 0-4-4Ts, leaving the description of the 6' 8" double-framed Dean and Churchward express passenger classes to a later Pen & Sword Locomotive Portfolio volume.

CHAPTER 1

THE ENGINEERS

DEAN AND CHURCHWARD

William Dean was born in 1840, the son of Henry Dean, manager of a London soap factory. He was educated at Haberdasher's School in New Cross and in 1855 he was apprenticed to Joseph Armstrong, then Locomotive Superintendent of the Great Western at Stafford Road Works, Wolverhampton. He shone at mathematics and physics and advanced rapidly, becoming Armstrong's chief assistant when still only twenty-three years of age. Armstrong moved to Swindon as Chief Locomotive, Carriage and Wagon Superintendent on the retirement of Sir Daniel Gooch in 1864 and left Dean in charge of Wolverhampton Works. Dean moved to Swindon in 1868 and became Chief Assistant Superintendent there until Armstrong's early death aged just sixty-one in 1877.

Dean was appointed in his place at the age of 37 and held office for exactly twenty-five years and had over 13,000 men under him at Swindon itself, plus enginemen all over the GWR system. He became a Justice of the Peace there and was highly respected both by his staff and in the community as a caring manager and public-spirited. He was a generous philanthropist and keen supporter of the Volunteer Movement. Already since 1868 a full member of the Institute of Mechanical Engineers, in 1878 he attained a similar rank in the Institute of Civil Engineers. As well as his broad gauge and standard gauge locomotives, he was renowned for his competence and forward thinking on both carriage and wagon design. He was a very practical man and aimed for simplicity, economy and easy maintenance of his rolling stock.

Despite his outstanding professional career, he suffered a tragic personal life. His first wife died soon after the birth of their third child and his second wife died after just eleven years of marriage. He also outlived both his daughters, one of whom died in infancy. By the 1890s, his own health had begun to deteriorate and by 1896 or so, his mental health began to crumble as dementia set in. Churchward was appointed as his assistant in 1897 and had the very delicate task of supporting him during his final years in theoretical charge as the Company, after so many excellent years of service, was reluctant to terminate Dean's career. Churchward conducted this difficult role with great sympathy and sensitivity and

William Dean, 1840 – 1905, Chief Locomotive Engineer of the Great Western Railway, 1877–1902. (GW official photograph)

George Jackson Churchward, 1857–1933, Locomotive Superintendent (1902–16) and Chief Mechanical Engineer (1916-22) of the Great Western Railway.
(GW official photograph/ NRM Collection)

final five years or so, was born in 1857 in Stoke Gabriel on the River Dart between Kingswear and Totnes and joined the South Devon Railway at Newton Abbot in 1873. After absorption of that railway by the Great Western in 1876, he transferred, aged just nineteen, to the Swindon Drawing Office and after a few rapid promotions was appointed as Carriage and Wagon Works Manager in 1885. Ten years later, he became Swindon Works Manager and identified as Dean's successor when he became his Chief Assistant in 1897, at a salary of £900 a year. Although he was not appointed as Locomotive Superintendent until 1 June 1902 – with his salary increased to £2,500 – he had been developing his ideas within the ample scope given him by Dean, and had already written a paper on a scheme for a limited number of 'standard' loco-motive designs by January 1901, although in the interim he maintained a steady production of Dean designed engines, albeit showing an increasing influence of his own ideas, especially boiler design.

The 1901 paper outlined a scheme for six standard locomotive classes, a 2-8-0, two 4-6-0s, a 4-4-0, a 2-6-2 tank, and a 4-4-2 tank. The first 4-6-0, No. 100, later 2900, was built within a month of Churchward's formal appointment and the 2-8-0, No.97, later 2800, was the second standard locomotive to emerge from Swindon Works in June 1903. By 1905, he had amassed sufficient experience of these prototypes to proceed with confidence and the standard 4-6-0s, 2-8-0s and 2-6-2 tanks began to be

many of the late developments of both the small and large wheeled 4-4-0s at the end of the century owed much to Churchward building on Dean's basic earlier designs. He eventually retired in 1902 aged 63, much revered in Swindon despite his failing health, and moved to a house in Folkestone, bought for him

by the GWR Company. He died in 1905 aged sixty-six. The respect showed to him was indicated by the fact that a street in the shadow of Swindon Works was named after him during his lifetime – in fact a good fifteen years before his death.

George Churchward, his successor and virtual co-manager during the built in quantity. Only then did the building of double-framed passenger 4-4-0s cease. Churchward finalised his plans for the full range of standard locomotives to meet all the Great Western Railway's needs, which, as well as the passenger locomotives, included the 2-6-0 mixed traffic 4300, which would cover the traffic needs that the small-wheeled 4-4-0s were still meeting. Its introduction in 1911 eliminated the need to build further 'Bulldog' 4-4-0s.

Churchward interested himself in locomotive, carriage and wagon matters, leaving the rest to his Chief Assistant, F.G. Wright. Churchward selected bright young engineers, involved them in frequent discussions, talked regularly to the draughtsmen and was active in seeking the views of practical men in the Works and running sheds, as well as maintaining his interest in developments overseas. The 1950s Western Region Chairman, Reggie Hanks, an apprentice himself at Swindon Works in 1912, recounted a couple of anecdotes about Churchward's hands-on involvement. On one occasion on Frome station, he observed the fireman leaning far out over the cab's side to see the injector overflow. He promptly had the overflow pipe moved from behind to the leading edge of the cab steps, so that the fireman did not have to lean out so far. On another occasion he was discussing some detail of design with his Chief Draughtsman and one of the younger office staff who had prepared the detailed work. The Chief Draughtsman began to answer Churchward's questions, but was told brusquely to 'Shut up – let the young man speak for himself. He did the work!' In such ways, Swindon design developed step by step and it put the Great Western a decade or more ahead of any other railway in the country as far as locomotives were concerned.

Churchward had an even temperament and a dignified bearing suggesting a 'country squire', strengthened by his interest in country pursuits, especially fishing. But he was also a good administrator and leader of men. He drew out the best from his staff and created a culture of good teamwork, a tradition and practice he inherited from Dean and his predecessors. In 1916, his title was changed to that of Chief Mechanical Engineer, he was awarded the CBE at the end of the war and in October 1920 he was the first Honorary Freeman of Swindon, of which he'd been the first Mayor as far back as 1900.

It is well known that his life ended run down by one of his successor's engines whilst crossing the line from his home to the Works, nearly twelve years after his retirement. He had retained his interest to the end and kept himself abreast of developments without obviously interfering with the policies and decisions of his successor. When he retired in 1922, the *Railway Magazine* had published a tribute, which included the words, 'It would be invidious to suggest that Mr G.J. Churchward CBE, who retired from the position of Chief Mechanical Engineer of the Great Western Railway, is the greatest locomotive engineer in modern British practice.'

Behind this reputation were a number of significant facts – he had established a fleet of 888 new locomotives, his passenger and freight locomotives had been compared against those of other railways and had been shown to shine in both performance and economy, influencing design of the other major companies. Locomotives to his basic designs were still being built more than a generation later and were at the forefront of Western Region power at nationalisation in 1948, although by then Dean's double-framed 4-4-0s and Churchward's developments of them were almost extinct. His early designs developed from the Dean double-framed engines had been completely eclipsed and although good and successful in their day, performing widespread secondary duties efficiently enough, most were withdrawn from service by the mid-1930s, superseded by Collett's mixed traffic developments of Churchward's basic standard 4-6-0 designs.

CHAPTER 2

THE DUKES
DESIGN & CONSTRUCTION

Dean's 2-2-2 No.10, the prototype Dean express engine using the Stroudley designed valves and arrangement of the Stephenson link motion that became a standard element of the later Dean 4-4-0 locomotives.
(GW Trust)

In the first few years of Dean's reign as Chief Locomotive, Carriage and Wagon Superintendent, most of his activity was on carriage and wagon matters, though in 1883 he produced the first 'Dean Goods', a remarkably successful 0-6-0 tender goods engine that went on to have many members, a long life, overseas War Department roles and was even found in the 1950s at Swindon to have bested an Ivatt LMS Class 2MT 2-6-0 when the latter was on test to improve its steaming capacity. Then the impending end of the broad gauge brought a number of problems re-equipping the new standard gauge routes with suitable motive power, retaining and converting the more recent of the broad gauge machines. Indeed, Dean actually designed and constructed a number of 'convertibles'.

In 1886 he built an important engine, a 2-2-2, No.10, with slide valves located under the cylinders and Stephenson's link motion, a piece of machinery invented by Stroudley on the London Brighton & South Coast Railway. This was the first GW locomotive with that valve gear and motion, which Dean then applied to his subsequent designs.

His first production passenger engines were large wheeled 'singles', 2-2-2s, numbered 3000–3030, built in 1891-2. 3021-3028 were actually constructed as broad gauge 'convertibles' and were indeed rebuilt for the standard gauge in 1892. 3000–3020 and 3029-30 were built for the standard gauge.

They were fast locomotives but one, 3021 *Wigmore Castle*, became

Dean 'Single' 2-2-2, No.3006 *Courier*.
(MLS Collection)

derailed at speed in Box Tunnel in September 1893 with a number of injuries. Their stability at speed with only a pony truck to guide came under investigation and despite his reluctance to countenance four wheel bogies at the front end, Dean turned to four 2-4-0s, three broad gauge and one standard gauge, which had been relatively unsuccessful and did little work. Nos. 7 and 8 had been experimental compound machines, No. 7 standard gauge, and No. 8 broad gauge. The other two broad gauge engines, Nos. 14 and 16, were 'simples'.

Dean overcame his prejudice against four-wheel front bogies and rebuilt these four engines completely in 1894 as standard gauge 4-4-0s

with 7' 1" coupled wheels and large 20" cylinders. They were handsome locomotives, known as the 'Armstrong' class after the name bestowed to No.7, but were

disappointing on the road and Churchward rebuilt them between 1901 and 1911 with various types of boilers that he was developing. They were renumbered 4169-4172 when

The 1886 built Dean 'compound' 2-4-0, No.8, in original condition.
(MLS Collection)

The 1888 Dean 2-4-0 'simple' No.14, built as a broad gauge 'convertible', in original condition.
(MLS Collection)

Former Dean compound 2-4-0 No.8, rebuilt by Dean as a 7' 1" 4-4-0 in 1894 and named *Gooch*.
(Bob Miller Collection/MLS)

Former Dean 'simple' 2-4-0 No.16, rebuilt in 1894 as a 4-4-0 and named *Brunel*, seen here at speed on Goring troughs with an up express, c1900. (Bob Miller Collection/MLS)

Dean rebuilt 4-4-0 No.8 Gooch, subsequently reboilered by Churchward and renumbered 4172 (in the post 1912 number series of the 6' 8" Dean/Churchward outside-framed 4-4-0s).
(Bob Miller Collection/MLS)

The handsome Dean 'single' 4-2-2, 3077 *Princess May*, at Westbourne Park, Paddington. An Armstrong condenser 0-6-0T is in the background, c1900.
(Bob Miller Collection/MLS)

later converted to 6' 8" 'Flower' class between 1911 and 1923, and were withdrawn between 1928 and 1930.

With the successful bogie conversions and the 1893 experience of the Box Tunnel derailment of his express 2-2-2, Dean converted 3000–3029 to 4-2-2s and built the capable 4-2-2s that brought GW performance over the level routes of London–Bristol–Exeter to a new high.

With the experiments and developments of the express passenger locomotives of 1891 – 1894 behind him, Dean turned this experience to the problem facing the company of providing suitable power for the Newton Abbot–Penzance heavily graded route which had been the last section of GW broad gauge converted in May 1892. As early as 1891, Dean was aware of the need, as services west of Newton Abbot had been left in the hands of a motley group of broad gauge tank engines, mainly 4-4-0 and 0-4-4 side and saddle tanks.

The outline design of a 4-4-0 tender engine incorporating the Stroudley/Stephenson cylinder and motion layout but with 5' 7½ " coupled wheels was completed in 1893 and the prototype, 3252 *Duke of Cornwall*, emerged new from Swindon Works in May 1895, at an estimated cost of £1,800 (roughly £135,000 at 2016 prices).

3252 had two 18" diameter x 26" stroke cylinders, a total heating surface of 1,398sqft, grate area of 19.11sqft and an axle-load of 15 tons 7cwt on the coupled wheels and 17 tons 10cwt on the bogie axles. The boiler, a lengthened version of the

successful 'Dean Goods' boiler (the S2), was pressed at 160lb and had a flush round-topped firebox, large brass dome and an extended smokebox to encompass a diaphragm plate and netting for spark arresting. This was possibly Churchward's influence and could well have been a response to the hot summer of 1894 when the GWR received many claims from Devon farmers following fires emanating from hard-working locomotives. It had Mansell wood-centred carriage wheels on both bogie and tender.

Dean 'Single' 4-2-2 3069 *Earl of Chester* at speed with a Bristol–Paddington express near Hayes, c1905.
(Bob Miller Collection/MLS)

A Bristol & Exeter Railway broad gauge 4-4-0 saddle tank No.2047, built in 1867, of the type used for services west of Exeter before conversion to standard gauge.
(Bob Miller Collection/MLS)

One of the former Broad Gauge 'convertible' '3521' class 0-4-2Ts rebuilt as an 0-4-4T to improve stability and used for services in Cornwall prior to the introduction of the 'Dukes'. Note the heavy weight on the wheel fixed to attempt to further improve the riding of the engine. (Bob Miller Collection/MLS)

A Standard Gauge outside framed 0-4-4T of the '3521' class, of the type used for passenger services in Devon and Cornwall before the advent of the 'Dukes' and before conversion by Churchward as a 4-4-0. (GW Trust)

The tender was short with a 11' wheelbase, to fit turntables in the West Country which until then had been required only to fit tank engines, and had a water capacity of 2,000 gallons. The engine weighed 46 tons and tender, 24, giving a total engine weight of 70 tons. The light axle-weight meant that the 'Duke' class was later categorised as 'yellow' route availability, which was the reason that a number of the class were retained much longer than many younger engines on routes – especially in mid-Wales – that were not permitted for heavier axle-load locomotives. Tractive effort at 85% was 16,848lb. Slide valves

with 4⅝″ travel were arranged below the inclined cylinders and screw reverse was fitted. The locomotive had curved double-frames, the inner frame joggled inwards behind the bogie. Inner and outer frames were ¾″ thick. The bogie had 'swing-hanger' suspension. It initially had steam sanding gear. Frames, valves and bogies were similar to those fitted to the four 'Armstrong' locomotives and the Dean 'Singles', with a pedigree back to Dean's 2-2-2 No.10.

3252 *Duke of Cornwall* reboilered with a Belpaire firebox and with curved nameplates as seen in the early 1920s.
(J.M. Bentley Collection)

3252 *Duke of Cornwall* as built in 1895. Note the builder's plate fixed to the frame.
(MLS Collection)

3253 *Pendennis Castle* as built in 1895 with straight nameplates on the boiler side. It is fitted with front bogie brakes (which were later removed).
(J.M. Bentley Collection)

3253 *Pendennis Castle*, the second 'Duke' (the class was initially known as the 'Pendennis Castle' class) as built in 1895. Its name was removed when 'Castle' 4079 was built and named in 1924.
(GW Trust)

The locomotive was finished in the elaborate black and orange lined green livery of the Great Western with the GWR scroll on the tender. The nameplate was straight and fixed to the boiler barrel between the smokebox and large dome and the brass numberplate was high on the cab side level with the cut away curve of the driver's look-out. The frames, wheel centres and splashers were painted 'Indian Red' (a reddish-brown) and the boiler, cab and tender the GW middle chrome green.

3252 was followed by 3253-3261 the same year, all receiving names associated with Devon and Cornwall, many from the Arthurian

3255 *Cornubia* as built in 1895, later renumbered 3254, and in 1946, 9054, which lasted until withdrawal in 1950. (GW Trust)

legends. The second engine to appear, 3253 *Pendennis Castle*, for some reason became the class name for several years, although the name was removed when 'Castle' 4079 received the name in 1924, the term 'Dukes' becoming the common epithet in the interim period. 3262–3276 followed in 1896 and 3277–3291 in 1897. The first twenty cost £39,300 against an authorised budget of £36,000 (£2.6 million in today's currency) and the second twenty a very similar £39,000, against an increased budget of £40,000. All

3256 *Guinevere* at Oswestry depot with Cambrian 4-4-0 1014, after both had double-headed a freight terminating at that location. It has had a topfeed fitted and has a short wheelbase Armstrong tender. (JM Bentley Collection)

3257 *King Arthur* with Belpaire firebox, topfeed and curved nameplates as in the early 1920s. Note the high position of the numberplate on the cabside.

(JM Bentley Collection)

continued to receive names associated with the West Country, many place names, some of which were removed later as there were complaints that some passengers mistook them for the destination of the train!

There was an interruption then as Dean turned his attention, supported by Churchward, to the needs of the main line express passenger business, as loads were increasing and although the Dean 'Singles' were excellent fast engines, their haulage capacity was limited. So the

6' 8" 'Badminton' class was created, similar in many other ways, but there were two experimental variants from the standard class, 3297 *Earl Cawdor* with a large boiler and enlarged and enclosed cab and 3310 *Waterford* with (probably under Churchward's influence) a Belpaire firebox and an enlarged domeless boiler. He also had a similar boiler fitted to three of the Dean 4-2-2s, including 3015.

Then, at the end of 1898, another 'Duke' was constructed, numbered 3312 and named *Bulldog*. It had a

Churchward boiler, prototype of what became the Swindon Standard No.2 boiler, although with a dome. The total heating surface was increased to 1,520sqft and the grate area was a larger 23.65sqft. The boiler pressure was 180lbpsi, the axle-load over the coupled wheels was 17 tons 6 cwt and the engine weight had increased by just over three tons. The wooden centred bogie and tender wheels were replaced by conventional steel centres. Tractive effort was now 18,955lb. The cab was also different and a screw reverse

3281 *Fowey* as constructed, renumbered 3272 in 1912, name removed in 1930 and withdrawn as 9072 in June 1949. (MLS Collection)

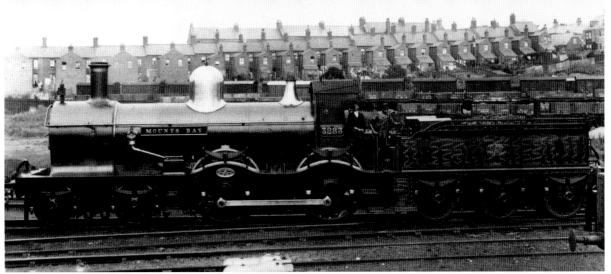

3283 *Mounts Bay* as constructed and in a highly polished condition, at Weymouth, c1900. Some drivers instructed the cleaners to make patterns with tallow on their engine, as here on the tender – the practice was known as 'guivering'. It was renumbered 3273 in 1912, then 9073 in 1946 and was withdrawn in December 1949. (GW Trust)

Badminton 6' 8"
wheeled 3297 *Earl Cawdor* built experimentally with the large boiler designed by Churchward's assistant F.G. Wright.
(MLS Collection)

Dean 'Single' 3015 *Kennet* fitted by Churchward with a domeless boiler and raised Belpaire firebox, c1905. Note the curved brass strip on the front of the cab, also the 'slots' on the bufferbeam and front handrail for the headlamps.
(Bob Miller/MLS Collection)

replaced the steam operated reverse system of the earlier 'Dukes'.

This was followed in 1899 with a further batch of standard 'Dukes', 3313-3331, also with a mixture of old broad gauge locomotive and West Country names. Again some were removed because of duplication with later engines, especially the 'Castle' class. There were detail changes slightly increasing the weight, 2,500 gallon capacity tenders with water pick-up apparatus, and the last four, 3328-3331, received raised Belpaire fireboxes. Prior to 1900, all the Duke locomotives shared their class number with the boiler number they

3312 *Bulldog* as constructed in 1898 with experimental parallel boiler and Belpaire firebox.
(GW Trust)

3312 *Bulldog* before rebuilding in 1906 with a tapered boiler, but with its straight nameplate replaced by the standard GW curved plate.
(GW Trust)

3322 *Mersey* as built in 1899. It was rebuilt as a 'Bulldog' in November 1907 and renumbered 3314. It was withdrawn in 1934.
(MLS Collection)

carried. After the Churchward standardisation much interchange of boilers between locomotives took place and the boiler numbers were not changed.

In 1903, the Churchward domed flush Belpaire boiler (B4) was standardised and gradually replaced the other types, the first being put on 3315 *Comet*. The last of the original S4 type boilers was not removed from 3279 until 1917. The raised

domed Belpaire boilers from 3328–3331 were also replaced, the last being on 3291, removed in 1913. The most efficient and effective of the Churchward boilers seemed to be the coned/tapered boiler with the high Belpaire firebox, giving a number of advantages over earlier types – increased steam space, an enlarged water line area, improved water circulation and the ability to remove the dome and its potential

weakening of the boiler barrel. An interesting development in 1904 was the fitting of 3346 *Tavy* with a mechanical stoker, although later it was transferred to a locomotive of the 'Atbara' class.

In 1902 3273 *Armorel* received a standard No.2 tapered boiler and in effect became one of the fleet of 5' 7½" wheeled engines that were later known as 'Bulldogs'. The first one built with a parallel No.2 boiler

3316 *Isle of Guerney*, built in 1899, with Belpaie firebox and with curved nameplates at Swindon, rebuilt as a 'Bulldog' in 1908, renumbered 3312 in 1912 and withdrawn in April 1931. (GW Trust)

3314 *Chepstow Castle*, built in 1899, renumbered 3282 in 1912, name removed in 1923 ready for 'Castle' 4077 and incorporated in 'Dukedog' 3216 (later 9016) in 1937. Note the high smokebox headlamp bracket and the short wheelbase tender. (GW Trust)

3266 *St Ives* (named removed in 1930), renumbered 3262 in 1912, incorporated in 'Dukedog' 3215 (9015) in 1937. Note the large cab forward window, the parallel boiler with raised Belpaire firebox, the filled-in short length fender on the tender and the builder's plate on the frame.
(GW Trust)

was 3352 *Camel* in October 1899 and was followed out of sequence by 3332-3337 that year and a further thirty-four of that class (3338–3351, and 3353–3372) in 1900. The 'Duke' 3312 named *Bulldog* received the Swindon No.2 boiler in 1906 and thus became a 'Bulldog' as well and gave its name to the whole class (initially they were known as the 'Camel' class). A further eighteen 'Dukes' were rebuilt as 'Bulldogs' between 1906 and 1909, leaving exactly forty 'Dukes' with the smaller B4 boilers as the increased boiler size, weight and axle-load pushed the 'Bulldogs' up into the next route availability 'blue' category. Superheating was introduced in 1911 and 'Duke' boilers gradually received this

St Ives after renumbering 3262 in 1912, with the same short wheelbase tender, and retaining the large cab window, but with addition of the topfeed, c1925.
(GW Trust)

additional modification over many years, the majority in the 1920s, but 3270 *Trevithick* was not superheated until 1944. About half the 'Duke' boilers were fitted with top feed from 1913 onwards. The straight nameplates were exchanged for the curved pattern over the front coupled wheel from around the end of 1903. Detail differences in appearance occurred in cab shape and cab window shapes. Piston valves replaced the slide valves from 1915 and some engines acquired shorter chimneys. From 1930, standard Churchward 3,500 gallon tenders, coal capacity 6 tons, were attached to some 'Dukes' and

3265 *Tre Pol and Pen* with Belpaire firebox as operating in the 1920s before withdrawal and rebuilding with 'Bulldog' frames to form the prototype 'Dukedog' in January 1930.
(J.M. Bentley Collection)

3275 *St Erth* (name removed in 1930), previously 3285, incorporated in 'Dukedog' 3203 (9003) in 1936, seen here at Plymouth in the early 1920s.
(Alan Gilbert Collection/MLS)

3283 *Comet*, seen here at Swindon, numbered 3315 prior to 1912, renumbered 9083 in 1946 and withdrawn in December 1950. (MLS Collection)

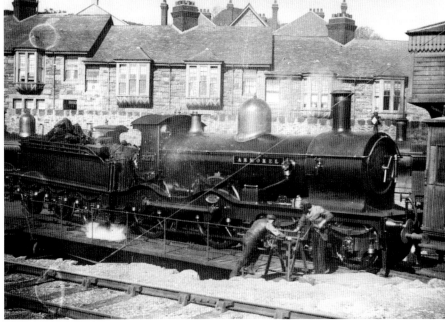

3273 *Armorel* built in 1896 before rebuilding with a new boiler in 1902 and becoming in effect a prototype 'Bulldog', seen here on one of the short wheelbase turntables at Penzance, where a projecting couple of 'spurs' held the protruding tender wheels clear during the turning movement. (GW Trust)

the cab sides were curved slightly outwards to be flush with the wider tender to avoid undue draughts causing coal dust to swirl. Automatic Train Control (ATC) was fitted to most engines of the class in the 1930s. In 1912, the GWR renumbered its locomotive fleet and the 'Dukes' retained roughly the same group of numbers but rationalised, removing those locomotives that had been rebuilt as 'Bulldogs'. The remaining forty 'Dukes' took the numbers 3252–3291, giving up their numbers in the 3300 series to the 'Bulldogs'. Only 3252 retained its original number as 3253 was one of the locomotives rebuilt as a 'Bulldog', becoming 3300, all subsequent numbers from 3254 moving up

3272 *Amyas*, built in 1896, with curved nameplates, renumbered 3266 in 1912, incorporated in 'Dukedog' 3215 (9015) in 1937. It still retains the old short wheelbase tender but note the way the coal has been piled high to increase capacity. (GW Trust)

places to cover the gaps caused by the twenty rebuilds. Like other GW locomotives, the 'Dukes' enjoyed a variety of liveries. The engine number was painted on the bufferbeam after 1900, and from 1903 the wheel splashers were green instead of Indian Red and a green line was inserted in the centre of the black and orange lining. During the First World War the 'Dukes' were repainted in a khaki green with black frames, then a plain unlined green until the railway amalgamation of 1923. For the rest of the GWR 's existence, the middle chrome green livery returned, lined

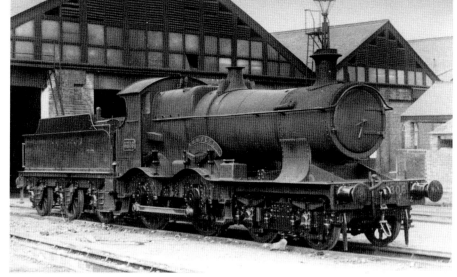

3273, rebuilt with Swindon Standard No.2 taper boiler as the first 'tapered boiler 'Bulldog', 3306 *Armorel*, at Swindon shortly before withdrawal in January 1939. (GW Trust)

3316 *Isle of Guernsey*, showing the curved nameplate fitted after 1903. 3316 was renumbered 3312 in 1912, was rebuilt as a 'Bulldog' in 1908 and withdrawn in April 1931. (GW Trust)

3324 *Quantock* photographed between 1903 when it received curved nameplates and 1908 when it was rebuilt as a 'Bulldog', renumbered 3315 in 1912, and withdrawn in June 1931. (GW Trust)

in black, green and orange, with black frames, wheels, smokebox and cab roof, with copper cap chimney and brass safety valve covers, although the dome was now painted rather than polished brass. The GWR monogram on the tender was replaced after 1904 by the lettering 'Great Western' being separated by the GW crest, which in turn was replaced by the GW 'shirt-button' roundel in the 1930s and just plain GWR during the Second World War until nationalisation.

In January 1930, 3265 *Tre Pol and Pen* was withdrawn because of fractured frames and at the same

3258 *The Lizard* at an unknown location, c1930. (GW Trust)

3267 *Cornishman* at Didcot, 8 March 1936. (M Yarwood/GW Trust)

3264 *Trevithick* at Tyseley, 14 September 1934. (GW Trust)

3276, formerly *St Agnes*, later 9076, at Old Oak Common, 19 October 1935.
(John Hodge Collection)

time a 'Bulldog', 3365 *Charles Grey Mott* was withdrawn, but the latter engine's frames were in good condition. Because of the need to retain sufficient 'yellow' route availability engines for some of the Welsh lines, the 'Duke' boiler was fitted to the 'Bulldog' frame and the 'Dukedog' class was foreshadowed – see Chapter 5. Twenty-nine of the 'Dukes' were withdrawn and converted to 'Dukedogs' between 1936 and 1939 and the eleven remaining engines survived the war to be renumbered in the GWR 1946 exercise in the 90XX series, retaining their last two digits – 9054, 9064, 9065 (the former *Tre Pol and Pen* now in effect a 'Dukedog'), 9072,

3266 *Amyas* at Didcot, September 1934.
(GW Trust)

3271 *Eddystione*, formerly 3278, at Machynlleth shed. It was incorporated with the frames of 'Bulldog' 3439 as 'Dukedog' 3204 in 1936 and was one of the last survivors, as 9004, withdrawn in 1960. (GW Trust)

3255 *Excalibur*, formerly 3256, at Swindon after intermediate overhaul, incorporated in 'Dukedog' 3205 (9005) in 1936. (G. Coltas/Bob Miller Collection/MLS)

9073, 9076, 9083, 9084, 9087, 9089 and 9091.

The first 'Duke', 3252, was withdrawn in August 1937 after completing 1,054,247 miles in traffic and its boiler, cab and motion amalgamated with the frames of 'Bulldog' 3434 to form 'Dukedog' 3214, later 9014, one of the last two to be withdrawn in October 1960, the reconstructed engine running a further 504,706 miles. The second 'Duke', 3253, was rebuilt as a 'Bulldog' in 1912 and was withdrawn and cut up in January 1936, having run 1,337,808 miles.

3268 *Chough* formerly 3275, rebuilt with Bulldog frames in 1939 as 'Dukedog' 3225 (9025). (GW Trust)

Unnamed 'Duke' 3280, formerly 3291 *Tregenna*, after the nameplates were removed in 1930, at Newbury, 24 February 1939. Its parts were incorporated in 'Dukedog' 3227 (9027) later that year. Note the autotrain in the background for the Lambourne Valley, converted from a former steam railcar. Note also the 'yellow' route availability circle has been applied to the cabside. (GW Trust)

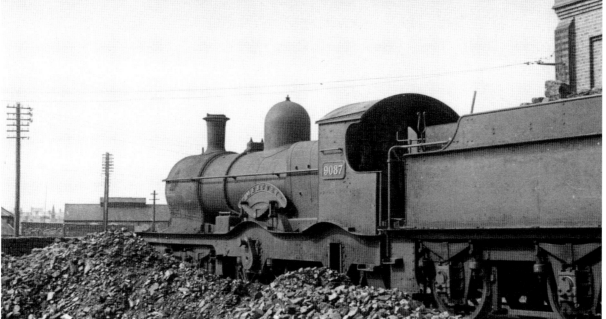

9064 *Trevithick*, former 3270 built in 1896 and renumbered 3264 in 1912, just before withdrawal in 1949. (GW Trust)

9087 *Mercury*, former 3321 built in 1899, renumbered 3287 in 1912, stored, partly dismantled, and awaiting withdrawal at Aberystwyth, 26 August 1948. Note unusual position of cabside numberplate. (GW Trust)

'Bulldog' 3434 in 1937 shortly before withdrawal and whose frames were used with parts from 3252 to form 'Dukedog' 3214.
(GW Trust)

3252 *Duke of Cornwall* at Didcot , 26 March 1926.
(John Hodge Collection)

After nationalisation the surviving engines were painted plain black with the BR 'lion & wheel' totem on the tender. Most were withdrawn in 1949, but 9054 *Cornubia* and 9083 *Comet* lasted to 1950 and the last two survivors, 9084 *Isle of Jersey* and 9089 (unnamed but formerly *St Austell*) were condemned in April and July 1951 respectively. All the 'Dukes', with the exception of 3285, and 3265 before reconstruction, ran more than a million miles – the highest mileage by a single 'Duke' was 9054 withdrawn in June 1950 (built in 1895 as 3255, renumbered 3254 in 1912) at 1,632,815.

'**Dukedog**' 3214 at Swindon, constructed from 3252 and 3434, at Swindon in 1939, some eighteen months afterwards. It was allotted the name *Earl Waldegrave*, never carried but later placed on 'Castle' 5057. As 9014, it was one of the two last withdrawn in October 1960.
(Bob Miller Collection/MLS)

3284 *Isle of Jersey*, formerly 3317, renumbered 9084 in 1946 and withdrawn in April 1951. (GW Trust)

9089, the last 'Duke' survivor, formerly 3326 *St.Austell* (name removed in 1930), renumbered 3289 in 1912, seen here at Gloucester on 26 April 1947, and withdrawn from Machynlleth shed in July 1951.
(GW Trust)

9072, built as 3281 *Fowey* in January 1897, renumbered 3272 in 1912, name removed in 1930, seen here at its home depot, Machynlleth, 30 July 1948, before withdrawal from the sub-shed at Aberystwyth in June 1949. Note that the smokebox lamp bracket has been lowered to give easier access, and that – despite the late date – no topfeed has been added.
(GW Trust)

9054 *Cornubia*, the last 'Duke' known to have worked a passenger train and the highest mileage engine of any of the doubled-framed small-wheeled 4-4-0s, arriving at Barmouth with a stopping train from Machynlleth, July 1948. 9054 was withdrawn two years later in June 1950.
(MLS Collection)

Former Bristol & Exeter Railway 4-4-0 saddle tank, No.2125, built in 1866, of the type that worked in Devon and Cornwall in the Broad Gauge era prior to 1892, and scrapped after the line west of Newton Abbot was converted to standard gauge.
(MLS Collection)

OPERATION

The 'Dukes' were expressly designed for the GW mainline in Devon and Cornwall after its conversion to standard gauge in 1892. The Dean 'Singles' had worked from Bristol to Newton Abbot, the engine change-over point, handing over to 0-4-2, 0-4-4, and 4-4-0 tank engines west of that point, often double-headed. From the outset, the 'Dukes' were known as the 'hill-climbing engines'.

The contemporary 4-2-2 Dean 'Singles' were not really capable of handling the gradients.

When the 'Dukes' arrived the engine change point soon moved to Exeter, as the smaller wheeled engines were better able than the Dean 'Singles' to accelerate trains round the speed restricted coastal line, with the slowings to exchange tokens for the single line sections

through the Parson's Rock Tunnels, with many of the trains stopping also at Teignmouth and Dawlish. The severity of gradients on the Newton Abbot–Plymouth section is well known, with the fearsome Dainton Bank, 1 in 36 at its steepest westbound, followed by the climb from Totnes to Rattery Box, and Hemerdon a longer but relatively straight 1 in 42 eastbound. However,

Cornwall is full of gradients ranging between 1 in 50 and 1 in 70, with track curvature preventing trains getting a run at the banks.

Before the summer of 1890, there were only four trains daily running from Paddington to Cornwall, and the quickest of them was the *Flying Dutchman* (11.45am from Paddington) conveying first and second class passengers. In 1898, there were seven such trains, all conveying first, second and third class passengers. For several years the passenger traffic to and from Cornwall had been increasing and there was need for a better service. From the summer of 1890, the GWR introduced an accelerated service departing Paddington at 10.15am, formed of corridor coaches. This was the *Cornishman*, calling only at Swindon, Bristol, Exeter and Plymouth, thence to Penzance, which was reached at 7.00pm.

The GWR took over the refreshment room at Swindon station, the stop at that station was withdrawn and the train still further accelerated to Plymouth. It left Paddington at 10.35am, called at Bristol and Exeter, and arrived at Plymouth at 3.53pm. The journey of nearly 247 miles was performed in 5 hours 18 minutes. In 1896, the popularity of the *Cornishman* was such that the train ran in two portions. These were at 10.30 and 10.35am, both corridor trains, each being composed of eight or nine exceptionally comfortable eight-wheel bogie coaches.

There is a record of a run by a 'Duke' in the summer season of

1897. It was a relief express, the 10.35am from Paddington to Falmouth and Newquay, non-stop over the 194 miles to Exeter. Charles Rous-Marten decided to investigate and he wrote about it in the *Railway Magazine* of March 1898. The six-coach train was hauled by 'Dean Single' 3029 *White Horse* as far as Exeter, a distance of 193¾ miles, accomplished in 3 hours 36 minutes and 25 seconds, notwithstanding ten bad signal and track relaying checks. The arrival was five minutes before time. At Exeter, 3289 *Trefusis* ('one of Mr. Dean's new 'pullers'') took over. *'There is a marked air of 'bull-dog' determination about this type of locomotive. The idea is suggested that whatever may happen, it will pull the train through somehow. And it usually does.'* After leaving Exeter, it had to wait at Dawlish for three minutes for the up train, which had not come off the single line at

Parson's Rock Tunnel. It passed Newton Abbot at high speed, and climbed strongly at 25mph up the Dainton Incline, passed at 60mph through Totnes, and worked hard up Rattery Bank, this time at 21mph. It ran at 60–65mph between Ivybridge and Cornwood and would have been a minute early into Plymouth but for a signal check outside the station. The 52 miles from Exeter took 73 minutes net. The Newquay portion of the train was separated at Par Junction. The train arrived at Falmouth at 6.13pm, two minutes before time. 3268 *Tamar* had charge of the return journey bringing three bogies from Falmouth and picking up the other three from Newquay at Par. Train weight was 150 tons and Hemerdon Bank brought the speed down to just 13mph at the summit and Dainton reduced it to 16mph but it was still a minute early into Exeter where 3029 took over again.

The first of the standard gauge outside framed 0-4-4Ts built by Dean for the GW in Devon and Cornwall around 1888-9, originally built as 2-4-0Ts but rebuilt as 0-4-4Ts to give extra stability.
(GW Trust)

A view of 3253 *Pendennis Castle* in service at Plymouth North Road a few days after construction and entering service in May 1895. The original elaborate livery is seen here to advantage. Note the coal piled high on the 2,000 gallon tender. (GW Trust)

As early as 1895, the 'Dukes' were involved in the running of the Ocean Mail specials from Plymouth Docks to London. The first left on 28 November 1895 from Plymouth Millbay at 7am, consisting of five vehicles with a tare weight of just 121 tons. 'Duke' 3256 *Excalibur* worked the train as far as Exeter, where it handed the train over to a Dean 4-2-2 for the onward run to Paddington via Bristol. 3256 would have been coupled to the train at the dock gates and then run non-

stop to Exeter. Three weeks later, the prototype *Duke of Cornwall* was the train engine, with Laira Driver Sutton. These trains were recorded and published in the *Railway Magazine* by the well-known train timer, Charles Rous-Marten, and both covered the 32.7 miles to Newton Abbot in 44 minutes and the 52.9 miles to Exeter in 68 and 66 minutes respectively, the latter engine being a little speedier round the coastal section. Even at the height of the post 1904 Ocean Mail

races with the LSWR, the Plymouth–Exeter time did not come below 66 minutes. Unfortunately, Rous-Marten did not quote the speeds sustained on the climbs to Hemerdon and Dainton, but the average speed over both runs to Newton Abbot was just over 44mph and there was little scope for fast running downhill because of the curvature – the 'Dukes' rarely exceeded 55–60mph. On the second recorded run, 4-2-2 3040 took over at Exeter

3254 *Boscawen* brings a Newton Abbot–Exeter train round the estuary to Teignmouth running in shortly after construction, c1895. Note the remnants of the former Broad Gauge 'baulk road' track retained after the 1892 conversion.

(J.M. Bentley Collection)

3253 *Pendennis Castle* on a down West of England service, near Aller Junction before the climb of Dainton Bank, c1896. (GW Trust)

A pair of 'Dukes' 3277 *Earl of Devon* leading and train engine 3255 *Cornubia* doublehead the *Cornishman* (Paddington–Plymouth–Penzance) train out of Newton Abbot, past the Works, 1903. The first vehicle is a mail van. (GW Trust)

3326 *St Austell* with Belpaire firebox enters St German's station in Cornwall with the Plymouth–Penzance portion of the *Cornish Riviera Express*, equipped with new 'concertina' carriages in 1906.
(J.M. Bentley/Real Photographs)

3257 *Guinevere*, piloted by a Dean 4-2-2 rebuilt with a Swindon standard boiler on a London train west of Exeter, c1902. (GW Trust)

3282 *Mounts Bay* (with large cab spectacle window) hurries round the coastal stretch between Teignmouth and Dawlish with an up express, a postal sorting van at the front, 1908. (GW Trust)

and 3046 at Bristol arriving Paddington at 11.17am, the mails being delivered to the General Post Office before midday.

On Tuesday 24 October 1899, a special train left Paddington at 8.15am for Plymouth, with passengers for a steamer of the Hamburg-America line. The train stopped only once at Exeter. A week later, the train was hauled by 4-2-2 No.3076 *Princess Beatrice* as far as Exeter, arriving at 11.53. 'Duke' 3331 *Weymouth* took over there, departing at 11.59. The train passed Newton Abbot at 12.27 and it reached Plymouth (Millbay) Docks on time at 13.30.

After making many journeys west of Exeter on various classes of locomotive including the later

3287 *St Agnes* (with the standard round cab spectacle window) also with what appears to be a same or similar postal sorting vehicle behind the tender, on the sea wall between Teignmouth and Dawlish, c1908. (J.M. Bentley Collection)

3313 *Cotswold* drops down Rattery bank passing Tigley signalbox after assisting a train over the South Devon banks, c1910. The up track is standard, but the down track retains the former Broad Gauge 'baulk road' form. Note the two young girls beside the track – taking lunch to their father, the signalman perhaps? The 9-lever Tigley Box opened in May 1908 and closed in June 1964.
(J.M. Bentley Collection)

3328 *Severn*, built with a Belpaire firebox, pauses at Teignmouth with an up stopping passenger train, 1902.
(J.M. Bentley Collection)

'Bulldogs' and '3521' 5' 2" wheeled 4-4-0s, Rous-Marten summarised his experience thus:

'All did very satisfactory work, but as the entire Cornish system is a series of sharp reverse curves and excessively severe grades, often 1 in 50 to 1 in 60, it is obvious that the work is necessarily of a plodding or 'hard-slogging' nature, very useful, but not attractive to the general reader in respect of detail. The doughty small-wheeled engines showed some excellent pulling up the steep banks, but owing to the sharpness of the curves they were debarred from attaining any really high speeds on the descending

grades. As a rule they ran down the steep hills with steam off and a frequent touch of the brakes. They were rarely allowed to exceed a maximum of 50 to 55 miles an hour. Nor, in view of the strong lateral movement often experienced in the tail end of the train in turning the numerous sharp curves, can this precaution be deemed other than prudent. ……I fear we can hardly look for an average speed greatly in excess of 30 miles an hour west of Newton Abbot….."

Looking at times recorded by Rous-Marten, the author O.S. Nock surmises, by comparing these times with his own later recordings, that normal speeds at Hemerdon summit would probably be about 15mph and Dainton, 18mph. Times and speeds were very similar to later times recorded by 4-6-0s in the 1920s,

though with then substantially heavier loads.

The strenuous work in Devon and Cornwall was already having consequences. As early as 1897, one

of the first 'Dukes', 3253 *Pendennis Castle,* received a new boiler after only running 63,000 miles and patch repairs were made to the frame which was already beginning to

3273 *Armorel* is turned on a short turntable at Penzance – the tender is held clear during the turning movement resting on the two spurs tilted to clear obstructions.
(GW Trust)

The 'Dukes' also hauled freight trains. Here, 3281 Fowey heads a freight, c1905. Note the high position of the front headlamp, and the coal piled high in the small tender.
(J.M. Bentley Collection)

3269 *Tintagel* with a down express in the Acton area, c1903. The train is composed of Dean gas-lit clerestory coaches.
(GW Trust)

3258 *King Arthur* on a local passenger train, at Liskeard, c1903. The first vehicle is a Dean brake van.
(GW Trust)

show cracks – a problem that the 'Dukes' and the curved frame 'Bulldogs' later both suffered from. The glamorous work of the 'Dukes' was comparatively short-lived, as within five years of their introduction, the 'Bulldogs' took over the most prestigious working west of Exeter. They did of, course, find slow passenger and fast freight working among their duties in the west, but by the end of 1900, eighteen had been transferred to the Paddington Motive Power Division and in 1901, the first 'Dukes' had been transferred to Pontypool Road in South Wales. By 1904, that depot

3261 *Mount Edgcumbe* with a down express composed of Churchward 70' 'concertina' rolling stock, nearing Bristol in the St Anne's Park area, c1910. The signal box is believed to be East Depot No.1 opened in February 1909.

(Bob Miller Collection/MLS)

OPPOSITE:
3279 *Tor Bay* with a Newton Abbot–Exeter stopping train at Dawlish, c1912.
(J.M. Bentley Collection)

had as many as twenty-two for operations on the 'North & West' route (Cardiff/Bristol to Hereford and Shrewsbury). The *Railway Magazine* of June 1898 included an article on the development of the Welsh holiday resort, Tenby, and the running of a 10.45am Paddington to the resort, regularly hauled by one of the Dean 'Armstrong' 4-2-2s, usually *Gooch* or *Charles Saunders*. It was scheduled to Bath (107 miles) in 120 minutes and then went up Filton Bank and through the Severn Tunnel (the Badminton route had not yet been opened) arriving at Newport at 1.55pm, where engines were changed. Motive power west of Newport through to Tenby would, after 1901, have been one of the South Wales 'Dukes', arriving four hours later at 5.55pm.

In 1900 the following allocations are known:
Devon & Cornwall (Exeter, Newton Abbot, Plymouth (Millbay), Truro, St Blazey, Penzance) – 3252, 3253, 3255, **3256**, 3261, 3264, **3268**, 3269, 3271, **3272**, **3274**, **3278**, **3281**, 3282, 3283, **3285**, 3287, **3288**, **3290**, 3314, 3315, **3318**, 3319, 3320, 3321, 3325, 3326, **3327**, 3328, 3329, **3330** and 3331, a total of 32.
Paddington Division – 3256, 3257, 3260, 3263, 3267, 3268, 3270, 3272, 3273, 3274, 3278, 3280, 3281, 3285, 3286, 3288, 3289, 3290, 3318, 3324, 3327 and 3330.

There is some duplication highlighted in 'bold' above as these 'Dukes' were transferred from the Newton Abbot Division to Paddington during 1900. It will be noted therefore that the West of England allocation had already dropped from thirty-two to twenty by the end of the year, caused by the influx of later small-wheeled 4-4-0s, the 'Bulldogs'.

Also by this time, 3258 had been transferred to Pontypool Road. Further transfers to South Wales began on 18 January 1901 with 3274, which moved on further from Paddington. By 11 May 1904, a total of twenty-two had been transferred. Every single one of the Paddington 1900 engines listed above had found their way there. In O.S. Nock's book *Fifty Years of Western Express Running* (Edward Everard, 1954) he records a day's survey undertaken at Paddington station by the late A.V. Goodyear on Saturday July 2 1904. It is of interest that no 'Duke' turns were noted at all, despite

3276 *St Agnes*, renumbered from 3287 in 1912, on a down express at Dawlish in 1912.
(J.M. Bentley Collection)

the plethora of other 4-4-0s – 'Badmintons', 'Atbaras', 'Cities' and 'Camel' 5' 8" engines and even members of the 5' 2" '3521' and 2-4-0 'Barnum' classes. The London Division based engines listed earlier had already gone to work trains on the North & West and South Wales and had been replaced by 'Camels' ('Bulldogs') on London trains to Reading, Weymouth and semi-fast trains to Swindon and Cardiff.

Other transfers before renumbering in 1912 were:
Wolverhampton Division – 3260, 3275, 3319, 3322 and 3329.
Swindon – 3266. 3312 *Bulldog* was there from new.
Weymouth – 3257 and 3267.
Salisbury – 3316 and 3317.
Hereford – 3291 and 3328.
Gloucester – 3313.

By 1913, over half the class had been taken away from the West Country and during the 1920s and 1930s new work was found for them. Most were then found at Didcot (a large contingent, working to Newbury and Southampton), a few at Banbury and Tyseley (working to Stratford), eight at Reading, working to Basingstoke, Swindon and Oxford, twelve at Gloucester including the Hereford and Ledbury branches, thirteen at Swindon covering especially the former M & SWJR, and the largest contingent (finally thirty-three) working the former Cambrian lines in Central Wales. The specific reallocations were in the period from 1913 until the start of the Second World War:

Didcot –	1913 – 1918 (approx): 3253, 3284, 3290.
	1920s: 3278, 3254, 3255, 3263, 3272, 3274, 3282 and 3289.
	1930s: 3254, 3256, 3266, 3274, 3280, 3282, 3283, 3285, 3290 and 3291.
Banbury –	3263, 3281, 3286.
Gloucester –	1910s: 3257 , 3290.
	1920s: 3252, 3261, 3268, 3271 and 3287.
	1930s: 3260, 3264, 3278, 3285 and 3289.
Tyseley –	3258 (1917 – 1930) 1930s: 3281 and 3284.
Reading –	1920s: 3254, 3275, 3276, 3279, 3285, 3286, 3288, and 3290.
Swindon –	1920s: 3252, 3258, 3260, 3263, 3270 and 3287.
	1930s: 3253, 3269, 3278, 3279, 3288, 3289 and 3291.
Central Wales Division –	1922-3: 3254, 3259, 3260, 3261, 3269, 3270, 3276, 3280 and 3290.
	1924: plus 3256 and 3271.
	1925: plus 3264, 3277 and 3291.
	1926: plus 3252.
	1927: plus 3273, 3282 and 3287.
	1928: plus 3258, 3263, 3275 and 3283.
	1929: plus 3262 and 3271.
	1930: plus 3265 (newly rebuilt as the prototype 'Dukedog' after trials at Swindon).
	1931: plus 3255, 3257.
	1932: plus 3253, 3272 and 3287.
	1933: plus 3284 and 3288.
	1934: plus 3268.
	1935: plus 3289.

3323 *Mendip* at Acton, c1900.
(GW Trust)

3322 *Mersey* awaiting its next duty, at Wolverhampton Low Level, c1905.
(GW Trust)

3258 *The Lizard* with a Manchester Exchange–Chester train, with a milk van behind the engine, 31 May 1913. (GW Trust)

3253 *Boscawen* on Swindon shed, 11 September 1932.
(J.M. Bentley Collection)

Unnamed 3261, previously 3265 *St Germans*, on the turntable at Cheltenham St James, whilst working over the former M&SWJR to Swindon and Andover, April 1933.
(Bob Miller Collection/MLS)

3260 *Mount Edgcumbe* at Wolverhampton Low Level. (J.M. Bentley Collection)

3261 *St Germans*, before removal of its nameplate in 1930, at Southampton Terminus. (J.M. Bentley Collection)

3284 *Isle of Jersey* (renumbered 9084 in 1946 and one of the last survivors that reached nationalisation) passes Twyford with an Oxford–Paddington semi-fast service in the 1920s. An early non-corridor Collett coach has been sliced into a Dean 4-car clerestory set. The sixth vehicle is also a Collett coach with a Dean 40' brake vehicle at the back. A three-coach Dean non-corridor clerestory set is in the centre road siding. (J.M. Bentley/Real Photographs)

3278 *Trefusis* on Swindon shed, 2 June 1935.
(L. Hanson/J.M. Bentley Collection)

3280 unnamed, but formerly *Tregenna* on the 7.11pm Didcot, pausing in the bay at Newbury and working towards Winchester and Southampton, 6 June 1938.
(M. Yarwood/GW Trust)

3281 *Cotswold* on a freight on the Berks & Hants, c1925. The first two vehicles are NE coke wagons and the fifth is a 'Felix Pole' coal wagon.
(GW Trust)

3281 on an up freight at West Drayton, April 1922. The first six vehicles are 'Felix Pole' coal wagons.
(GW Trust)

3284 *Isle of Jersey* at Spring Road with a Birmingham
Snow Hill–Stratford-on-Avon service, 9 May 1939.
(GW Trust)

3257, formerly 3258 *King Arthur,* departs Dovey Junction with a train for Machynlleth and Welshpool, passing a Dean Goods 0-6-0, c1930. A Cambrian Railway non-corridor coach is the second vehicle behind the locomotive.
(MLS Collection)

3259 *Merlin* and another unidentified 'Duke' climb Talerddig Bank, c1925.
(GW Trust)

3280 *Tregenna* approaching Dovey Junction with a train for Aberystwyth, c1930. The train is a motley collection of vehicles including a Siphon Van, top-light full brake and third class coach, a Dean gas-lit 68' coach, and a Cambrian coach.
(J.M. Bentley Collection)

3271 *Eddystone* at Welshpool on the 9.58 from Whitchurch to Aberystwyth, 6 April 1926.
(Alan Gilbert Collection/MLS)

During this period, as seen from the tables on page 65, there was a steady migration, concentrating the 'Dukes' on the mid-Wales routes. All but seven of the un-rebuilt 'Dukes' were working over the former Cambrian Railway routes immediately before the rebuilding of twenty-nine of them with 'Bulldog' frames for continuation on the restricted infrastructure of those lines. Due to lack of finance, the Cambrian infrastructure, including bridges, especially the coastal stretch from Machynlleth to Portmadoc and Pwllheli, was designated a 'yellow' route by the civil engineer, only permitting the 'Dukes', a few surviving 2-4-0s, the 'Dean Goods' 0-6-0s and the small-wheeled '3521'

class (see Chapter 4). The Cambrian routes, like the Cornish lines for which the 'Dukes' were designed, had a number of severe gradients and a constant need to accelerate from slowings to exchange tokens, as the majority of the Cambrian main line was single with passing loops only (twenty-four in all!). The route has a good number of undulating sections but the severest tests for the engines were the climbs from both directions to Talerddig summit just east of Machynlleth. Westbound, the gradient extends for eight miles with sections of 1 in 71 and 1 in 80. From Machynlleth eastbound, there are six miles of 1 in 100, a mile of 1 in 60, then just over three miles of 1 in

52/56 to the summit. The load for the 'Dukes' unassisted was established as 238 tons over the Cambrian section as a whole, but 182 tons for the eastbound climb to Talerddig. When a 'Duke' was assisted by another 'Duke' or an assistant engine of equal power, 360 tons were allowed, and frequently needed for the heavy summer holiday trains bound for Birmingham or London.

A search for logs behind 'Dukes' in the records of the Railway Performance Society identified just two, both on Shrewsbury–Welshpool local services in the 1930s. On 3 December 1932, 3270, unnamed (the name *Earl of Devon* had been

removed), and still un-superheated, was at the head of five coaches, 151 tons, on the 2.30pm Shrewsbury to Machynlleth as far as Welshpool, the 19½ miles occupying 33 minutes 5 seconds. No speeds were recorded but of course there were slowings to exchange the single line token en route. 3270 was later rebuilt with the frames of 'Bulldog' 3390 as 'Dukedog' 3226, later 9026. A run in 1960 on the *Cambrian Coast Express* double-headed by a 'Manor' and a 63XX Mogul took 35 minutes 27 seconds, pass to stop with maximum speeds between token exchange of around 55mph, so one can assume similar speeds were made by 3270.

On 8 September 1937, 3273

3278 *Trefusis* heads a train of GWR large cattle wagons at Leamington Spa, 1929. (G. Coltas/MLS)

3256 *Guinevere* pilots Cambrian Railways Beyer Peacock
4-4-0 1014 into Oswestry with a freight, c1925.
(GW Trust/Real Photographs)

The prototype 3252 *Duke of Cornwall* at Welshpool with a Cambrian line passenger service in the 1930s. (J.M. Bentley Collection)

Mounts Bay was the motive power for the two-coach 10.30am Welshpool–Shrewsbury stopping train which trifled with the load, arriving at Breidden three minutes early and Westbury where it was four minutes early but had to wait to cross a down service. Leaving there 3¾ minutes late, it arrived in Shrewsbury after a one minute signal stand at Sutton Bridge Junction just 1¼ minutes late. 3273 remained a 'Duke', only being superheated in 1946 when it was renumbered 9073. It was withdrawn in December 1949.

During the Second World War, the surviving 'Dukes' were seen frequently on freight services in the

3257 unnamed, but previously *King Arthur*, departs Barmouth with a train for Harlech and Pwllheli, 1936. The second vehicle is a former Cambrian Railways coach. (J.M. Bentley Collection)

3270 unnamed, formerly *Earl of Devon*, at Portmadoc, 1935.
(MLS Collection)

3269 *Dartmoor* pilots a 'Dean Goods' 0-6-0 on a train at Borth, July 1936.
(J.M. Bentley Collection)

Acton–Reading–Oxford–Banbury area and on the Didcot–Newbury–Winchester route and they were also used on troop trains en route to Southampton Docks via that route. After the Didcot–Winchester route was upgraded for wartime traffic and larger engines were utilised, a couple were allocated to Stourbridge for the Severn Valley line and the rest were based at Machynlleth and Shrewsbury.

After the war, the remaining 'Dukes' eked out their final days in the Machynlleth area, with all eleven (including 3265 which was in effect a 'Dukedog' – see Chapter 5) just making the British Railways era.

3269 *Dartmoor* hurries a stopping train along the Didcot, Newbury and Southampton line, with a load of three Dean gas-lit clerestory coaches and GWR horseboxes in the 1930s.
(J.M. Bentley Collection/Real Photographs)

3259 *Merlin* at Barmouth with a local train for Dovey Junction and Machynlleth, 27 August 1937.
(John Hodge Collection)

3259 *Merlin* runs light over Barmouth Bridge, c1935.
(GW Trust)

3259 *Merlin* at Machynlleth with a local train for Welshpool, c1930. (GW Trust)

3268 *Chough* at Patricroft alongside a LNWR Bowen Cooke 0-8-2T, having arrived with an excursion from the Central Wales coast for the Railway Queen Carnival, 10 September 1938. (Bob Miller Collection/MLS)

3254 *Cornubia* pilots a 90XX 'Dukedog' on a holiday express leaving Aberystwyth, 7 August 1939.
(J.M. Bentley Collection)

3291 *Thames* leaving Aberystwyth with a portion of a summer Saturday holiday express to join with the Barmouth portion at Dovey Junction, c1939.
(GW Trust)

9084 *Isle of Jersey*, after renumbering in 1946, passes Llynclys (near Llanidloes) on a freight which includes an LNER cattle wagon (first vehicle) and two Midland cattle wagons (second and third vehicles).
(J.M. Bentley Collection)

9083 received the temporary 'W' suffix but none carried a smokebox numberplate. 3265 *Tre Pol and Pen*, the prototype 'Dukedog' although still classified as a 'Duke' being renumbered 9065, was withdrawn in December 1949 along with 9064 *Trevithick*. 9073 *Mounts Bay*, 9072, 9087 *Mercury* and 9091 *Thames* had gone earlier in the year, the last survivors, 9054 *Cornubia*, 9083 *Comet*, 9084 *Isle of Jersey* and 9089 all working in the Machynlleth–Barmouth area until their demise in 1950 and 1951. The last noted passenger working was with 9054 in 1949. After that date they mainly worked on local pick-up goods traffic.

9073 *Mounts Bay* at Ruscombe Sidings near Maidenhead with a freight, 8 June 1948.
(J.M. Bentley Collection)

3289 unnamed, but formerly *St Austell,* trundles a light pick-up freight at Southam near Cheltenham, May 1946.
(W. Potter/MLS Collection)

3287 *Mercury,* shortly to be renumbered 9087, at Welshpool marshalling a local freight, 12 August 1946.
(MLS Collection)

CHAPTER 3

THE BULLDOGS
DESIGN & CONSTRUCTION

As stated in Chapter 2, 'Duke' 3312, built at the end of 1898, was named *Bulldog* and varied from the standard 'Duke' construction in that its boiler was larger, the prototype of the Swindon No.2 boiler that was very much the initiative of Churchward rather than Dean. It had a raised Belpaire firebox and the straight nameplate was fixed on its side rather than on the boiler barrel as for the others of the class. In addition to the different boiler, the cab was extended forward to cover the screw reverse, replacing the steam reversing gear that was fitted to the early 'Dukes'. These variations increased its weight to 49 tons 4cwt and the axle-loading over the coupled wheels to 17 tons 6cwt, the same as on the bogie wheels. Another experimental variant by Churchward that influenced the design of the 'Bulldogs' was 6' 8" wheeled 'Badminton', 3310 *Waterford* which had a similar boiler to that of 3312, but domeless.

However, the first locomotive of the class that became known later as 'Bulldogs' was not 3312, but 3352 *Camel*, constructed in October 1899. It had curved frames like the 'Duke' class and a domeless boiler like that on 3310, but whereas that boiler was parallel, 3352 had the developed form of what became known as the Swindon No.2 boiler, with 277 tubes and increased heating area of 1,663.02sqft although the grate area was reduced to 21.45sqft compared with 3310's 23.65sqft (but larger than the 'Duke's' 19.11sqft). 3352 had the same wheelbase, bogies, 18" x 26" cylinders and motion as the 'Dukes' as well as the identical frame and could quite accurately be described as a 'Duke' with the Swindon No.2 boiler, the latter being pressed at 180lbpsi. The axle-load over the coupled wheels was slightly reduced

3312 *Bulldog* as first constructed in 1898, with the prototype Swindon No.2 boiler and raised Belpaire firebox. (GW Trust)

3310 *Waterford*, the 6' 8" coupled-wheel 4-4-0 of the 'Badminton' class that was built with a Churchward experimental domeless boiler that was developed for the 5' 8" 4-4-0s that followed, as built in 1898.
(Bob Miller Collection/MLS)

3352 *Camel* shortly after construction in October 1899. The numberplate is fixed to the side of the smokebox, which was restricted to this locomotive. Note the jack on the running plate.
(GW Trust)

from that of 3312, although at 16 tons 16cwt, more than the 'Dukes' which pushed it to a higher route availability classification, 'blue', which became of importance later and was why the 'Dukes' outlived most of the 'Bulldogs' by many years. The tractive effort at 85 per cent was 18,955lb and a 3,000 gallon capacity tender was attached which held four tons of coal. The cab design introduced by Churchward, whilst still relatively spartan, was much more geared to the comfort and ease of operation for the driver. The cab was much wider than the cramped Dean design, and the regulator could be operated by the

Another photo of 3352 *Camel* in original condition, at Slough, c1900.
(Bob Miller Collection/MLS)

3352 *Camel* with the combined number and nameplate as fashioned for subsequent members of the class, c1903.
(GW Trust)

driver in a sitting position – indeed, there was a tip-up seat. Previously, the driver had to stand to operate the regulator. Also the new cab had large forward spectacles through which the driver could see, again in a seated position. Externally, apart from the obvious difference of the boiler, 3352 was distinguished by a large brass numberplate being fixed either side of its smokebox and a large circular plate on the cabside encompassing both name and number. It was named *Camel* after the Cornish river.

It was immediately followed in January 1900 by a production batch of twenty more numbered 3332–3351, filling in the numerical gap between the last 'Duke' constructed and the

3338 *Laira* works photo as built in January 1900. (GW Trust)

3335 *Etona* at Reading, from the first production batch of 'Camels', built in 1900. The jack on the running plate is very clear here. (GW Trust)

prototype 3352. They continued the naming themes of the 'Dukes' using a mixture of West Country names with Greek mythology, any of the previous carried by broad gauge engines. There was then a pause of a couple of months in construction while Swindon once more turned to larger wheel express passenger locomotives, the 'Atbara' class.

Then, from May 1900, Swindon recommenced construction of the 5'

8" and 6' 8" engines at the same time, producing 3353–3372, this batch of twenty locomotives completed by the end of the year. The main and obvious difference to the earlier batch was the shape of the double-frames. Straight rather than curved frames were applied to the 'Atbara' class and the batch of smaller wheeled engines constructed at the same time shared the same design of frame. The running plate

was also straight but on two levels, being raised over the coupled wheels and cab, the step between the forward area over the cylinders and bogie and the rear section being curved. The names of the latest batch of locomotives were again a mixture, this time with Arthurian names as well as places, the latter suffering from their withdrawal later to avoid passenger confusion, as with some of the 'Duke' names. They also had

3348 *Titan* as built in March 1900. Note the cleaners' 'guivering' with tallow of the cab, frames and tender.
(GW Trust)

3355 *Camelot* as built in June 1900 at Weymouth.
(MLS Collection)

3357 initially named *Exeter* when built in June 1900, but renamed *Royal Sovereign* temporarily in 1902 for royal train duties west of Newton Abbot (the visit of King Edward VII and Queen Alexandra). The crown headlamp is now in the GW Society museum at the Didcot Railway Centre.

(J M Bentley Collection)

3357 *Smeaton* as renamed in 1903 after completion of royal train work the previous year.
(J M Bentley Collection/ Photomatic)

3368 *Sir Stafford* at Gloucester, 3 April 1906.
(J M Bentley Collection)

3413 *Edward VII* as built in December 1902 with parallel boiler and raised Belpaire firebox. Note the large size nameplate with full brass beading over the whole curve.
(MLS Collection)

the standard No.2 parallel boiler with raised Belpaire firebox.

Then, from December 1902 and throughout 1903, forty new engines of the 'Camel' class were constructed, the first, 3413, being named *Edward VII* in honour of the new king. The first twenty retained the parallel No.2 boiler, then the taper boiler was introduced on one of the 'Atbaras', 3405 *Mauritius*. Churchward described his development of the tapered boiler in a paper to the

Institute of Mechanical Engineers in 1906. This paper demonstrated the extent to which he had studied American practice, both the advantages and disadvantages of the wide firebox and its relevance to Great Western practice and needs. Some American boilers were coned, and Churchward began to experiment, but the cone was in from the rear section of the boiler next to the raised Belpaire firebox. He noted that less trouble had been

experienced with a flat top firebox, with its advantage of increasing the area of water line at the hottest part of the boiler. That, combined with a coned connection to the barrel, enabled the dome, often a source of weakness, to be dispensed with and drier steam obtained.

He presented his case particularly on the experience of the boilers on 3310 *Waterford* and 3312 *Bulldog*. From these, he developed the design on from the Swindon No.2 to the

3413 *Edward VII* seen at Oxford, 1904.
(GW Trust)

3414 *Albert Brassey* as built in December 1902, here with later 'coned' boiler. (MLS Collection)

3425 as *Sir W H Wills*, as built with parallel boiler in 1903. It was later renamed *Sir William Henry*. It is seen here at Westbourne Park depot, Paddington. (GW Trust)

3425 as renamed *Sir William Henry* but before acquiring a tapered boiler, thought to be seen here at Weymouth. (GW Trust)

No.4 boiler as on 3405. This 'tapered' boiler was coned for two-thirds of its length from 4' 10¾" of the parallel front ring to 5' 6" at the firebox tubeplate. The number of tubes increased from 277 to 350 of 1⅝" diameter, 1,818.12sqft of heating surface and 200lbpsi boiler pressure, though the grate area was slightly reduced to 20.56sqft. With the improved water circulation, Churchward was daring to build boilers with higher pressures, envisaging the possibility of 225lbpsi, just at the time other engineers were

nervous and reducing boiler pressures to economise. Churchward took great care to carry his drawing office, works and outdoor staff along with his ideas despite criticism in other quarters, and brought his theories into practice in the building of 3433 *City of Bath* in 1903. The boiler had a Belpaire firebox, with sides curving inwards at the top, the Standard No.4 being contemporary with his No.1 boiler on No.98, the prototype 4-6-0.

With this amount of thoughtful development work on the boilers, it

is surprising, perhaps even astonishing, that Churchward persisted with new designs incorporating double-frames. One can surmise, perhaps, that he did not want to risk trying to introduce too many innovations at once – problems that have hit subsequent railway innovations as diverse as Bulleid's 'Leader' class to the BR Advanced Passenger Train. His boiler developments took priority, the Dean frames were well tried, the works staff were familiar with them and had the appropriate expertise,

3417 *C.G. Mott* as built in 1903 and before the name was amplified to *Charles Grey Mott*. When this locomotive was withdrawn in January 1930 its frames were used for the rebuilding of 'Duke' 3265 as the prototype 'Dukedog'. This engine also has a very large nameplate with full brass beading.
(GW Trust)

3424 *Sir Charles Kingscote* at Swindon, which appears to have arrived on an annual excursion trip, with a group of visitors who appear to have dressed for some sporting occasion.
(GW Trust)

One of the first batch of 'Bulldogs' built with a Swindon No.4 taper boiler, 3445 *Ilfracombe*, built in September 1903 after the experimental provision of a taper boiler to 'Atbara' 3405 *Mauritius*, seen here at Weymouth.
(GW Trust)

and he did not move away from these designs until his new standard designs (4-6-0s, 2-8-0s and 2-6-2Ts) were thoroughly tested, in full production and operating reliably. Once the 'Saints' were clearly successful, he built no more 6' 8" wheeled double-framed 4-4-0s, and no more 'Aberdare' 2-6-0 freight engines once the 28XX 2-8-0s were the mainstay of the GWR's coal movement. He did not at that time have the works capacity to build a mixed traffic standard locomotive – that had to wait until 1911 when he introduced the 43XX 2-6-0. Therefore, he continued to allow Swindon Works to turn out the 'Camels', right up to January 1910.

3385 *Newport*, one of the 1903 batch of 'Bulldogs' built with the Swindon No.4 boiler, subsequently revived a No.2 boiler after renumbering in 1912 from 3447 to 3385, c1925.
(J Neeson/MLS Collection)

3389 *Taunton*, built in 1903 and renumbered in 1912 from 3451, name removed in 1930, at Old Oak Common.
(MLS Collection)

There was therefore another pause as Swindon was busy building passenger 4-4-0s and the first 2-6-2T, No.99. By October 1903, sixty 'Camels' had been constructed with a parallel version of the No.2 boiler, but the advantages of boiler interchangeability with the 'Atbaras' was attractive and frequent boiler exchanges took place. The 'Atbaras' had been built with the No.2 boiler, the barrel 11' long, half-cone (the later engines had three-quarter length coned boilers). In effect they were No.4 boilers with the same length firebox but a shorter barrel. They had 289 tubes of 1⅝" diameter,

3342 *Orion* at Swindon as rebuilt with a Standard No.2 taper boiler but before renumbering, c1910. (GW Trust)

1,396.58sqft of heating surface and what became a standard size GW grate area of 20.35sqft. Boiler pressure was 195lbpsi – thirty of the sixty ordered were constructed with these boilers.

1905 was taken up with construction of Churchward's new standard locomotive designs, but in March 1906 3312 was rebuilt with a three-quarter length cone No.2 boiler and from then on locomotives of the class were known as 'Bulldogs'.

Earlier, in February 1902, a 'Duke', 3273 *Armorel*, was rebuilt with a similar boiler and at that time there was a plan to convert all the 'Dukes' in this way. In fact, over its

forty-two year life 3273 (later 3306) managed to sport seven different boiler types at various periods – the flush round top when new, parallel domeless in 1902; half-cone No.2 in 1906; three-quarter-cone No.2 in 1910; half-cone No.2 superheated in 1912; three-quarter-cone superheated in 1914; and Standard No.3 in 1933!

After the conversion of 3312, eighteen more 'Dukes' were reboilered and became 'Bulldogs', starting with 3262 in October 1906 and finishing with 3330 in December 1908. By 1909, the class was 141 strong. The Swindon No.4 boiler became the standard for the new 6' 8" wheeled 'Cities' in 1903, and the

No.2 boiler was standard for the 'Bulldogs' from April 1904.

125 double-framed engines were built under Churchward's auspices between 1902 and 1910. Hairline cracks had begun to appear around the crank axles of double-framed engines three times more frequently than in single-framed engines. Frame strengthening was done by patch-repairing, especially of the larger wheeled locomotives. Was Churchward neglecting this area, by his attention being focused mainly on his new standard locomotives and the boiler developments he was initiating? The last double-framed engines were his 'improved

3311 *Bulldog* (previously numbered 3312) as rebuilt with tapered boiler and seen here after the 1912 renumbering, c1930.
(J M Bentley/Real Photographs)

3273 *Armorel* in its later guise as 3306 and rebuilt with Standard No.3 boiler post 1933.
(GW Trust)

3304 *River Tamar* rebuilt from Duke 3268 in June 1907, seen here with a Churchward 43XX mogul, at Old Oak Common, c1920s.
(GW Trust)

3307 *Exmoor*, a 'Duke' formerly 3279, rebuilt with taper boiler in December 1907 as a 'Bulldog'. The loading gauge in the photo is of LSWR design and suggests the location is Salisbury.
(GW Trust)

3308 *Falmouth* rebuilt from Duke 3280 in January 1909.
(Bob Miller Collection/MLS)

3309 *Maristow* rebuilt as a Bulldog from Duke 3282 in July 1907, seen here at Wellington in the early 1930s.
(GW Trust)

3313 *Jupiter*, rebuilt from 'Duke' 3318 in
February 1908, at Exeter St David's, c1925
(GW Trust)

3310 *St Just* rebuilt in September 1908 from 'Duke' 3286.
(MLS Collection)

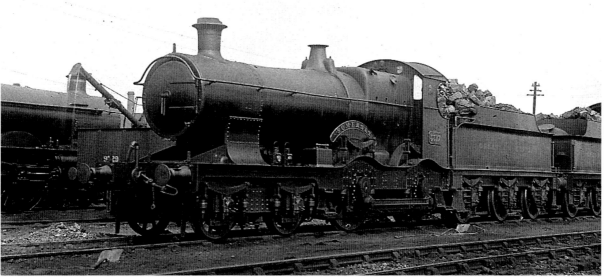

3317 *Somerset* rebuilt from 'Duke' 3327 in May 1908, at Old Oak Common, 16 May 1925.
(John Hodge Collection)

3733 *Chaffinch* built in May 1903 and seen here in Works grey, later renumbered 3443. Note the low position of the numberplate on the cabside.
(MLS Collection)

3743 *Seagull*, built in January 1910 and the class last survivor, withdrawn from Reading shed in November 1951.
(GW Trust)

3390 *Wolverhampton* (formerly 3452 and name removed in 1930) fitted with Westinghouse air brakes for working traffic from the former Great Central to the South Coast via the GW Banbury–Old Oak Common route, seen here at Old Oak Common, c1925.
(GW Trust)

Bulldogs' of 1909-10 with modified bogies, screw reverse and deeper frames – 3731-3735 of May 1909 and 3736-3745 constructed between November 1909 and January 1910. They were all named after birds and were the last 'Bulldogs' to remain in traffic, a handful surviving until nationalisation.

In December 1912, the GWR introduced a wholesale renumbering of its rolling stock, when the twenty 'Dukes' rebuilt as 'Bulldogs' received new numbers from 3300, the start of the 'Bulldog' number block, while the Dukes' remaining closed the gaps resulting from this. The smaller wheeled double-framed engines took the numbers in the 3200 - 3500 blocks, while the 'Cities' and 'Counties' moved to 37XX and 38XX respectively and the other double-framed 6' 8" wheeled engines were regrouped in the 41XX block. The revised numbers are given in detail in the appendix; suffice to say here that the 'Bulldogs' ran consecutively from 3300 to 3455.

During the next decade, changes took place in their outward appearance. Churchward was not enamoured of over-elaborate liveries and the standard GW livery applied to these classes was plain chrome green with black underframes, simplified lining and removal of the GWR 'scroll' on the tender sides. 3320-3360 had large oval combined name and numberplates on the cabsides and some engines were attached to 2,500 gallon tenders. Then from 3341 onwards, straight rather than curved frames and running plates became standard. It had been the intention to create 'Super-Bulldogs' by fitting them with the Swindon No.4 boiler, but these were allotted as priority to the high-wheeled express passenger engines. Despite this, boilers emerged pressed to a range of pressures, varying from 180 to 200lbpsi with all gradations in between – the latter higher pressure not on 'Bulldog'

3322 *Eclipse*, built in November 1899, at Old Oak Common, c1920s.
(Bob Miller Collection/MLS)

3321 *Brasenose*, built in November 1899, seen here at Stafford Road ex-works in GW green livery, 24 April 1932.
(H.C. Casserley/MLS Collection)

3322 *Eclipse* seen here at Worcester, c1933.
(MLS Collection)

boilers until 1919. However, there was a lot of interchange of boilers as the standardisation policy had made this easy to apply and some engines – for example 3366 and 3384 – actually reverted to parallel boilers after having been fitted with coned boilers.

Superheating was introduced on the 'Bulldogs' in 1909, most were converted between 1910 and 1912 and all were superheated by 1915. Top feed was fitted from 1911 and screw reverse was introduced once more on the 'Bird' series of 'Bulldogs'. New cylinders with piston valves were fitted from 1912 and all these changes were gradually

3323 *Etona* at Cardiff, c1930.
(John Hodge Collection)

3326 *Laira* at Reading in the 1920s, before being de-named.
(MLS Collection)

3340 *Camel*, the prototype Bulldog of October 1899, here rebuilt with taper boiler, at Reading, 13 March 1926.
(John Hodge Collection)

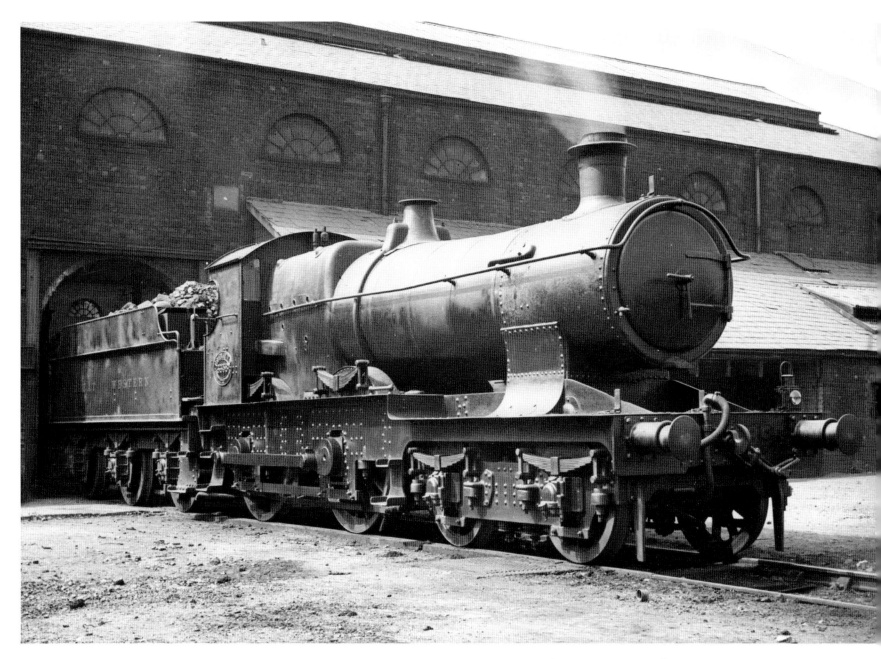

3358 *Tremayne* at Oxley, 14 August 1933.
(M.Yarwood/GW Trust)

3360 *Torquay* at Chester shed just before its name was removed to avoid passenger confusion, 1929.
(W.Potter/MLS Collection)

3361 unnamed, but formerly 3413 *Edward VII*, at Exeter, 28 September 1926.
(GW Trust)

3367 *Evan Llewellyn* with a 'County' 4-4-2T, thought to be at Reading, c1930.
(GW Trust)

3363 *Alfred Baldwin*, previously 3415 *Baldwin*, seen here at Newton Abbot in the late 1930s.
(GW Trust)

3375 *Sir Watkin Wynn*, c1930.
(GW Trust)

3379 *River Fal* seen here in the late 1930s.
(GW Trust)

3388 *Swansea* before name removal, on a turntable, c1920s.
(GW Trust)

3394 *Albany*, fitted with Westinghouse brake to run inter-railway trains from the Midlands to the South Coast, c1930.
(GW Trust)

3394 *Albany* with Westinghouse brake, stored here at Old Oak Common just prior to withdrawal in 1934.
(MLS Collection)

increasing the tractive effort of the engines to over 20,000lb. Tapered cast chimneys were fitted from 1920 and four engines (3434 in 1913, 3429 in 1914 and 3390 and 3394 in 1915) were fitted with the Westinghouse air-brake system to enable them to be coupled with foreign rolling stock on inter-railway workings. This was removed between 1931 and 1934. Surplus Standard No.3 boilers from withdrawn 36XX 2-4-2T, as they were relatively new, were used on fourteen 'Bulldogs' from 1933 – 3306/08/69/74/76/80/83/89/91/95 and 3400/28/30/52

3395 *Tasmania*, at Exeter, c1930.
(GW Trust)

3409 *Queensland* leaving Cardiff Central with an up train from platform 1 by the Central Hotel, c1930.
(John Hodge Collection)

3415 *George A Wills,* c1936.
(MLS Collection)

3425, unnamed, ex works at Swindon, c 1930. 3425's frames were later used for 'Dukedog' 3217/9017, now preserved on the Bluebell Railway.
(GW Trust)

3429, unnamed, and fitted with Westinghouse brake, c1930.
(GW Trust)

3434 *Joseph Shaw* at Reading, 1933, after removal of Westinghouse brake gear.
(GW Trust)

3433, unnamed at Swindon shed, 17 May 1937.
(GW Trust)

After 1925 there were more detail changes. ATC was fitted to most engines between 1928 and 1931. Cabsides were extended outwards at the rear to make them flush with new 3,500 gallon tenders (apparently the older cab shape with the wider 3,500 gallon tenders caused excessive draughts and eddies of coal dust).

Many 'Bulldogs' were withdrawn in the 1930s and as will be explored in more depth in Chapter 5, many were officially withdrawn but donated their frames to the rebuilt 'Dukedogs' with 'Duke' boilers to retain a sufficient fleet of 'yellow' route availability engines between 1936 and 1939. It was intended to renumber the 'Bulldogs' in the 8000 series in the

3448 *Kingfisher* at Didcot, 6 June 1937.
(Bob Miller Collection/MLS)

3448 *Kingfisher* at Didcot, 7 September 1935.
(R.K. Blencowe Collection/MLS)

GW 1946 renumbering scheme, but there were so few left by then that the remaining 'Birds' were left with their 1912 numbers and had been withdrawn before the numbers were utilised for some of the Hawksworth taper-boiled pannier tanks.

The first 'Bulldog' to be withdrawn was 3320 as early as August 1929; most went in the mid-1930s or were rebuilt as 'Dukedogs'. 3335 and 3378 were retained as war reserves and the last survivors were Reading's 3453 *Seagull* and 3454 *Skylark*, both withdrawn in November 1951. Total mileage run by individual machines varied from 850,000 to 1,463,000.

3453 *Seagull*, at Reading, c1930. A 'Star' stands as up line pilot on the adjacent track. (GW Trust)

3322 *Eclipse*, withdrawn in March 1935 and 3323 Etona, withdrawn in August, under demolition in Swindon Works, 13 September 1935. (GW Trust)

3451 *Pelican* seen here at Exeter in the closing months of ownership by the Great Western Railway, 30 September 1947.
(J D Davey/MLS Collection)

3377, formerly named *Penzance*, at Swindon Works after a light overhaul, 1948.
(MLS Collection)

3341, *Blasius*, one of the few Bulldogs fitted with a smokebox numberplate at Exeter St David's, 30 July 1949. It was withdrawn in November that year.
(F M Gates/GW Trust Collection)

3453 *Seagull* in its last days at Reading shed,
just before withdrawal in November 1951.
(GW Trust)

OPPOSITE:
The nameplate of 3454 *Skylark*. (GW Trust)
The nameplate of 3400 *Winnipeg*, the lower brass
beading damaged during the replacement of the outside
springs (a common occurrence). (GW Trust)

3447 *Jackdaw* on Swindon 'dump' awaiting scrapping, 24 June 1951. It had been withdrawn two months earlier.
(MLS Collection)

3371 *Tregeagle*, built in December 1900, passes Dawlish with an up express, 1901.
(GW Trust)

OPERATION

In the early days, the 'Camels' had replaced the 'Dukes' over the South Devon Banks. The 'Dukes' had reigned for barely five years in the West Country before most were transferred to London, South Wales and the North & West. In the first decade of the twentieth century the 'Camels' or 'Bulldogs', as they were known from about 1906 onwards, had almost total control of passenger work in Cornwall, and a substantial proportion between Plymouth and Exeter. The load limit for these engines west of Newton Abbot was eight bogie coaches, about 220 tons, and in summer much double-heading had to be resorted to – two 'Camels' or a 'Camel' and one of the remaining 'Dukes'. Schedules in Cornwall were an overall three and a quarter hours (193 minutes plus station time) for the 114.2 miles, split 58 minutes for the 34.7 miles from Plymouth to Par, 89 minutes for the 53.7 miles on to Truro, 27 minutes for the next 15.2 miles to Gwinear Road, 8 minutes for the 5 miles to St Erth and 11 minutes for the final 5.6 miles to the Penzance terminus. Similar overall times were allowed in the Up direction.

Charles Rous-Marten commenced his articles entitled *British Locomotive Practice and Performance* in the September 1901 *Railway Magazine* although there were few logs recorded for the 5' 8" wheeled 4-4-0s at this time – most interest was in the

3332 *Avalon*, built in November 1999, on a down express at Dawlish, c1902.
(GW Trust)

3310 *St Just,* rebuilt from Duke 3286 in 1908, passes Dawlish with an up express in 1912.
(J.M. Bentley collection)

3340 *Marazion* on a down express for Penzance passing Mounts Bay near its destination, c1902. The consist includes a horsebox, a full brake parcels van, and a GW 6-wheel coach.
(GW Trust)

TOP: An '00' gauge kit model of 3447 *Jackdaw* owned by the author. The livery of GW green plus early BR logo on the tender was a combination unlikely to have been seen in reality, although the prototype was not withdrawn until April 1951.
(David Maidment)

CENTRE: Bachmann model of 'Dukedog' 9022 owned by the author. (David Maidment)

BELOW: 9017 in BR plain black livery threads through Lindfield Wood on the Bluebell Railway with an engineers' train, 5 February 2010.
(Jonathan Bowers/Bluebell Railway)

ABOVE: 9017 in GWR green livery arrives at Horsted Keynes with a saloon special from Sheffield Park on the Bluebell Railway, 24 February 2008. Although in GW livery it bears the number 9017, which would be correct for the 1946-48 period only, after the renumbering and before nationalisation. (Jonathan Bowers/Bluebell Railway)

9017 doubleheading 3440 *City of Truro* arriving at Carrog at the Llangollen Spring Gala, April 2009.

(David Maidment)

ABOVE: 9017 arrives at Glyndyfrydwy station passing a Llangollen-bound train, during the Llangollen Railway Spring Gala, April 2009.
(David Maidment)

TOP LEFT: 9017 in BR black livery, but unnamed, at the Llangollen Railway Spring Gala, April 2009.
(David Maidment)

LEFT: 9017, at the Llangollen Railway Spring Gala, on arrival at Llangollen station from Carrog, April 2009.
(David Maidment)

9017 hauling a demonstration freight about to collect the single line staff for the section from Llangollen to Berwyn during the Llangollen Railway Spring Gala, April 2009.
(David Maidment)

9018 at Barmouth assisting a Collett 0-6-0, 2230, on a Birmingham-Pwllheli train, 2 August 1958.
(R.C. Riley Collection)

9025 having arrived at Swindon Works, and being withdrawn from traffic without repair, 25 August 1957.
(R.C. Riley Collection)

9004 in store at Wellington two months before official withdrawal, 23 April 1960.
(R.C. Riley Collection)

9004 in store at Wellington (rear view) two months before official withdrawal, 23 April 1960.
(R.C. Riley Collection)

9014 and 9017 head the Talyllyn AGM special on arrival at Towyn having powered the train over the Cambrian section, 26 September 1959.

(R.C. Riley Collection)

9015 on the Swindon 'dump' awaiting scrapping along with 2-6-2T 5150 and Hawkswoth pannier tank 9496, 6 November 1960.

(R.C. Riley Collection)

One of the two last survivors of the 'Dukedog' class
one month before its withdrawal, 9017 at its home
shed, Machynlleth, 7 October 1960.
(R.C. Riley Collection)

3456 *Albany*, built in 1904, at Plymouth North Road, c1905. A Mail sorting van is next to the engine.
(GW Trust)

large wheeled 'Badmintons', 'Atbaras' and after 1904, the 'Cities', especially when the GWR and LSWR began their competition with passengers and mails off the transatlantic liners docking in Plymouth. However, one was recorded by the Rev.W.J.Scott – April 9 1904, the first day of a 'race' between the GWR mails and LSWR passengers off the American Line *SS St Louis*. The motive power between Millbay Crossing and Exeter was 3452 *Wolverhampton*, of the 'Camel' class (later 3390) built just six months previously. 3452 and its five mail vans passed Newton Abbot in forty-seven minutes from Plymouth and reached Exeter in seventy-two

3340 *Marazion* at Brent with the 4.10pm Newton Abbot to Plymouth, 23 July 1910.
(John Hodge Collection)

3424 *Sir N Kingscote*, built in March 1903,
passing Dawlish on a down express, 1908.
(MLS Collection)

minutes, averaging 44mph over the South Devon Banks and the restricted running round the Dawlish coastline. With a 'City' 4-4-0 on to Bristol and Dean 'Single' 3066 on to London, arrival was seventeen minutes ahead of its rival at Waterloo, although that train had left Plymouth four minutes later. On subsequent 'race' days that were recorded the Plymouth–Exeter section was covered throughout by a 'City' class, which could cope with the heavy gradients with the light

load and was faster on the level and downhill, cutting the Plymouth–Exeter time to sixty-six minutes, and eventually to fifty-eight minutes, although Exeter was passed at speed as 3437 *City of Gloucester* was working right through to Bristol.

There was another record of a 'Camel' in Cornwall in 1903. A very special train – a 'royal' – much encouraged by the King, arrived in Plymouth behind 3433 *City of Bath* at the head of five coaches some thirty-seven minutes before time (allegedly

before the red carpet was down and the VIP reception party had assembled!). The train continued to Falmouth behind 3354 *Bonaventura* which covered the 47¾ miles to Grampound Road in sixty-nine minutes and stood there for seventeen minutes as it was running so early. At Truro it was early again and stood for five minutes. The train eventually docked in Falmouth in six hours seven minutes from London.

The GWR also had ambitions to build up Fishguard Harbour as a

3340 *Marazion* doubleheading a 'Small Metro' 2-4-0T on a Newton Abbot–Plymouth stopping train, 23 July 1910. (John Hodge Collection)

3349 *Lyonesse*, the 1900 built 3361, shortly after renumbering just before the First World War, at Penzance station with an up train for Plymouth, with modern stock including a Dean mail sorting van in chocolate lake (maroon) livery, c1912. The train will probably form an express for London after leaving Plymouth.
(GW Trust)

destination for Atlantic liners and the 'Camels' were allocated to some of the connecting boat trains west of Cardiff. Loads were heavy and either double-heading or the use of assisting engines round Cockett just west of Swansea was prevalent. An accident occurred on the approaches to the eastbound climb of Cockett Bank in October 1904, when the train 'Camel' engine, 3460 *Montreal*, was assisted on the front by an unsuitable 0-6-0 saddle tank, No.1674, which derailed unable to cope with the speed with which the two engines were charging at the 3 mile 1 in 50 gradient. The driver and the fireman of the saddle tank died and two passengers also from the crushing of the train behind the 4-4-0 which remained relatively undamaged on the track. Fifty passengers were injured and two died subsequently.

From 1904, there were sufficient 'Camels' for them to be spread throughout the GW system working secondary expresses and taking over from 'Dukes' on the Weymouth services. Some examples are given of the work by the 'Camels' in the survey of operations on 2 July 1904 at Paddington station, undertaken by A.V. Goodyear and mentioned in chapter 2. The 5' 8" 4-4-0s were noted on the following turns:

Down trains from Paddington –
9.35am to Southampton & Weymouth, 3333 *Brasenose*, 10 bogie coaches
9.45am to Reading, 3427 *Sir W. Wynn*, 8 bogie coaches + 2 other vehicles
11.40am slow to Cardiff, 3424 *Sir N. Kingscote*, 9 bogie coaches + 5 other vehicles
12.35pm to Weymouth, 3363 *One and All*, 9 bogie coaches
2.0pm to Oxford via High Wycombe, 3417 *C.G. Mott*, 11 bogie coaches + 1 other
2.40pm to Weymouth, 3466 *Barbados*, 5 bogie coaches

Up trains arrival times at Paddington –
9.32am from Swindon, 3424 *Sir N. Kingscote*
10.10am from Didcot, 3417 *C.G. Mott*, 10 bogie coaches + 1 other vehicle
10.55am milk train from Swindon, 3363 *One and All*, 5 bogie coaches + 5 tanks
2.47pm from Bristol via Devizes, 3425 *Sir W.H. Wills*, 4 bogie coaches + 2 other

3334 *Eclipse* on an up Weymouth service at Upwey, 1900.
(GW Trust)

Also of interest was the first reboilered 'Badminton' 3310 *Waterford* on the 9am *Torbay Express* and return on the 6.15pm arrival from Ilfracombe (which arrived 5 minutes early), and Churchward's prototype 4-6-0 No.98, which worked the 10.50am 2-hour fast service to Bristol, returning on the 4.30pm arrival Bristol express. The Weymouth services certainly seem to have been the preserve of the Bulldogs at this time.

In 1904, 3433 *City of Bath* replicated its royal run of the previous year and headed the inaugural run of a new Paddington–Plymouth–Penzance

3336 *Glastonbury* on an up Weymouth train about the time of the Paddington survey, c1904.
(GW Trust)

express named *The Inglishman* (in honour of the GWR Chairman, Mr Inglis ?). The six bogie coach train arrived in Plymouth in four hours twenty-four minutes and 'Camel' 3450 *Swansea* took over there gaining time steadily arriving at Truro seven minutes early and Penzance nearly fourteen minutes before time. 3450 also performed on the return run the next day and duly arrived at Plymouth a minute early, handing the train over to 3433 once again. In the 1901-1904 *Railway Magazine* articles *British Locomotive Practice and Performance*, Charles Rous-Marten devoted several issues to discussion of the comparative merits of express passenger 'single-wheelers' against the increasing use of four-coupled

engines. He seemed initially to be a devotee of the single-wheelers (he seems to have been a fan of the Dean 4-2-2s and their exploits between Paddington and Exeter), but he had to admit that when the GW Churchward 4-6-0s came on the scene, the argument in favour of the bigger engines was clinched.

The debate, at first, revolved round the decision of the GW to run non-stop to Plymouth via Bristol – Rous-Marten supported the previous policy of a Dean 'Single' to Exeter and a 'Camel' from Exeter to Falmouth and Par/Newquay. However, the authorities decided on a four-coupled 6' 8" 'Atbara' or 'City' to Plymouth which they deemed capable of mastering Dainton

and Rattery banks and the 'Camel' west of Plymouth only. A 1904 article describes a run with eleven bogie coaches from Paddington with one of Churchward's new two-cylinder 4-6-0s, the 'Atbara' 3388 *Sir Redvers* from Bristol to Exeter and 'Camel' 3429 *Penzance* piloted by 'Duke' 3277 *Earl of Devon* through to Cornwall. The 5' 8" coupled wheel pair took the heavy train in splendid style, running the fifty-two miles from Exeter to Plymouth non-stop in sixty-five minutes thirty-three seconds, topping Dainton at 28mph and Rattery at 24.3mph after a slowing through Totnes.

Rous-Marten and W.S. Scott analysed UK non-stop runs over 100 miles in 1904 and although the LNWR had the most (forty-two runs), the Great Western was second with thirty-one runs and average speeds ranging from 50-59mph. The LNW runs ranged from 49-56mph, the GNR twenty-four runs at 50-55mph and the Midland, eighteen runs at 51-54mph. All other railways had both fewer long distance non-stop runs and lower average speeds. However, the GW runs were with the 6' 8" wheeled engines, the 'Dukes' and 'Camels' taking over the slower extremities of the services among the hills of Devon, Cornwall and West Wales.

From 1911, the 'Bulldogs' found themselves being gradually displaced by Churchward's new 2-6-0 4300 class, which relieved them of their more important passenger and fast freight work and in particular began to take over the working of express trains west of Newton Abbot, including trains like the *Cornish*

3339 *Marco Polo* at Wolverhampton Low Level alongside an Armstrong outside-framed standard goods 0-6-0, c1902.
(J.M. Bentley Collection)

3368 *Sir Stafford* on an up semi-fast service from Bristol or Oxford to Paddington, on Goring Troughs, c1910. After the front full brake parcels vehicle, the second is a Broad Gauge 'convertible' coach.
(GW Trust)

3414 *Albert Brassey* with a down train at Swindon, c1910. Note the slip coach on the left.
(GW Trust)

3346 *Tavy* on a down semi-fast service near Acton, c1910.
(GW Trust)

3331 *Weymouth* at Paddington on a down express for Weymouth, shortly after rebuilding from a 'Duke' to 'Bulldog' class with a taper boiler in July 1907, c1908.
(GW Trust)

Riviera. In fact, however, the Bulldogs continued to do more passenger than freight work right up to the first withdrawals in 1929 and 1930. They were regularly used on semi-fast services in the Paddington-Reading-Oxford-Banbury route – one, 3327 *Paddington*, being used as the Reading station pilot covering failures requiring assistance in the up direction. During 1927, it was used on at least three occasions, once to help an ailing locomotive (a new 'King') on the *Cornish Riviera*. The Wolverhampton Division used them on fast freight work and Laira engines were sometimes used on

3345 *Perseus* passing Acton with an up semi-fast service including several early Dean milk vans, c1908. The Acton-North London line is in the background.
(GW Trust)

3419 *Evan Llewellyn* at Swindon with a stopping service from Bristol, c1910. Note the two former Broad Gauge 'baulk roads' in the centre.
(GW Trust)

3335 *Etona* with a Paddington-Bristol express approaching Bathampton, c1908. (GW Trust)

3459 *Toronto*, built in 1904, at Old Oak Common with a down semi-fast service consisting of Dean 4-wheeled close couple suburban coaches, c1905. (GW Trust)

3729 here unnamed, but later named *Weston-super-Mare*, renumbered 3439 in 1912, and de-named in 1930, on an express near Golden Hill Tunnel, between Pembroke and Pembroke Dock, c1906. (GW Trust)

3418 *Earl of Cork* at Paddington with a down express, c1905. Note the wooden platforms still in existence. The coaches are Dean 48' vehicles in chocolate lake livery.
(J.M. Bentley Collection)

perishable traffic during that commodity's peak season.

As mentioned earlier, finding recorded logs by 'Camels/Bulldogs' in the first decade of the twentieth century has been nearly as difficult as for the 'Dukes'. They worked in only Devon and Cornwall on express services in which train timers were mainly interested and there were many stops and heavy gradients

precluding any fast running. However, a few runs culled from the *Railway Magazines* of the 1909-14 period recount some 'Bulldog' performances. 3414 *A.H. Mills* was on a very lightly loaded Bristol-Wolverhampton train (85 tons) and charged up Filton Bank passing the summit in 6 minutes 20 seconds for the 3.2 miles from the Stapleton Road stop. Despite signal checks before

Standish Junction and approaching Cheltenham, it completed the 43 miles to that station in 53 minutes, 5 seconds and averaged 65mph between Charfield and Coaley.

A number of 'Bulldog' performances between Newton Abbot and Plymouth were logged and recorded. 3445 *Ilfracombe* on the 165 ton *Cornish Riviera Express* ran the 31.8 miles to Plymouth in a

3459 *Toronto* at Newnham Junction with a South Wales-Gloucester-Birmingham service, c1910. Note the horse, three plank ballast wagon and the coke wagon in the yard. (GW Trust)

minute and a half under the scheduled 44 minutes working up to 43mph beyond Aller Junction, the last mile to Dainton summit being run at an average of 30mph, and the subsequent climb of Rattery Bank was equally good with a minimum of just under 30mph. 3340 *Marazion* with 180 tons fell to 20mph approaching Dainton Tunnel but ran fast down the bank touching 60mph at Totnes. 3282 *Maristow* (a converted 'Duke') dropped a minute and a half on the schedule with 190 tons, whilst 3365 *Plymouth* assisted by 'Duke' 3319 *Katerfelto* with a heavy load of 355 tons beat the schedule by

3460 *Montreal* at Plymouth North Road ready to back a Plymouth portion onto an up Cornish express, c1910. (GW Trust)

3395 *Tasmania* departs Kingswear with a stopping train to Newton Abbot and Exeter, c1925. The River Dart is in the background.

(HC Casserley/Author's Collection)

3405 *Empire of India* enters Shrewsbury station with a local Wolverhampton - Chester train, 1933.

(AG Ellis/ML Boakes' Collection)

3417 *Lord Mildmay of Fleet* in Tyseley depot, 13.10.1935. (CFH Oldham - Lens of Sutton)

3449 *Nightingale* having assisted a King to Dainton summit, begins the descent down to Totnes with a Paddington-Plymouth express, c 1937.

(M.M. South/John Scott-Morgan Collection)

A named but unidentified 'Bulldog' pilots a 'King' over Dainton summit with the down *Cornish Riviera Express*, c1937.
(M.M. South/John Scott-Morgan Collection)

A nameless unidentified 'Bulldog' pilots at King
climbing Dainton Bank from Totnes with the up
Cornish Riviera Express, c1937.

(M.M. South/John Scott-Morgan Collection)

A 'Bulldog' and a 'Castle' clear Dainton summit and tunnel and begin the descent with a heavy Paddington – Plymouth express, c1937.
(M.M. South/John Scott-Morgan Collection)

3393 *Australia* pilots 4910 *Blaisdon Hall*, on an up Penzance-Paddington express at Gwinear Road, September 1933.
(I.C. Allan/GW Trust)

45 seconds. They were the fastest of all these timed trains up to Dainton, beating 3445's time from Newton Abbot by 15 seconds, with an estimated speed at the summit of over 30mph. Much later when the 'Kings' and 'Castles' took over train-engine duties, the 'Bulldogs' continued to give help as pilot engines over this difficult route.

In the reverse direction, the main interest was the ascent of the two mile 1 in 42 Hemerdon Bank. I have found accounts of three 'Bulldog' eastbound runs from Plymouth. The first, with a rebuilt 'Duke' 3318

3407 *Madras* leaving the Severn Tunnel and climbing to Patchway with a Cardiff – Bristol train, c1930.
(G H Soole/J.M. Bentley Collection)

Jupiter, undated but clearly before the end of 1912 when it was renumbered 3313, had 150 tons and made a fast start, passing Plympton at 60mph at the foot of the bank and cleared Hemerdon Box in 12 minutes 25 seconds with a minimum of 18mph. The second run with 3312 *Bulldog* itself and 175 tons was even faster passing Plympton nearly a minute quicker than 3318, but fell to 15mph at the summit of the climb, albeit with an extra coach. 3348 *Titan* (later 3336) had 285 tons and was assisted up to Hemerdon Box by 'Duke' 3265 *St Germans*, and the pair made an exceptionally fast climb, passing Plympton in just 5 minutes

10 seconds at 67mph and stopping at the summit signalbox in 10 minutes 30 seconds start to stop for the 6.7 miles – this is a good two minutes before any of the other runs passed Hemerdon summit! Unfortunately, the timer did not note the minimum speed before slowing to detach the pilot, but it must have been in the upper twenties.

Just one run is recorded west of Plymouth with rebuilt 'Duke' 3325 *St Columb* (later 3316). The engine had a 7-coach 215 ton train and ran the 34.7 miles from Plymouth to Par in 53 minutes 30 seconds, just a minute and a half slower than the 'Castle' hauled *Cornish Riviera*

Limited was allowed in the late 1930s. The first four miles took 8 minutes 40 seconds including the slowing over the Saltash bridge, then averaged 46½mph on to St Germans and sustained 36mph up the long climb (1 in 61/74/58) to Doublebois. After that speed was restrained averaging no more than 52-53mph down through Bodmin Road to Lostwithiel and the Par stop.

A number of 'Bulldogs' were based in the Newport Division at both Newport Godfrey Road (before Ebbw Junction shed was built) and Pontypool Road. A Pontypool Road Driver, John Drayton, described in his book *Footplate Years* how as a young boy living then in Newport, he would accompany his father to view rows of polished engines lined up beside the station – a Sunday morning when the shed was full was particularly popular and he told of the regulars – 3341 *Blasius*, 3371 *Sir Massey Lopes*, 3382 *Cardiff*, 3385 *Newport*, 3407 *Madras*, 3441 *Blackbird*, 3443 *Chaffinch* and 3451 *Pelican* as well as a quartet of the large-wheeled 'Flower' class 4-4-0s.

In the First World War, there was heavy traffic on the North & West route via Hereford and Shrewsbury and although the normal power was a 'County' 4-4-0 (a 'Saint' 4-6-0 after 1916) a couple of runs in the early war years with 'Bulldogs' exist. 3323 *Etona* (the post 1912 number), admittedly with a light load of 130 tons only, made a spirited run from passing Pontypool Road to the Hereford stop in 40 minutes 30 seconds (the 2pm Plymouth-Manchester in 1963 was allowed 42 minutes for 'Castle' haulage and

remained the same initially with Brush Type 47 diesels). The performance, with unusually high speeds of 70mph before the Penpergym slowing and 74mph at Pontrilas (a 60mph line restriction there in 1963) plus a minimum speed of 31mph at Llanvihangel, was very similar to a five coach run on the 2pm Plymouth with double chimney 4087 *Cardigan Castle* in April 1963 – the only stretch on which the 'Castle' was faster was on the ascent of Llanvihangel which 4087 cleared at

46mph. The second run was with 3399 *Ottawa* (formerly 3461) with 225 tons after amalgamating the Bristol and South Wales portions at Maindee North Junction (Newport). However, this was slower and took 47 minutes 40 seconds, a time more comparable to the normal running of the heavier 1963 4pm Plymouth-Crewe passenger and mails when steam replaced diesel traction temporarily in the spring of 1963.

The advent of the Collett 'Halls' in 1929 had a ripple effect on the

'Bulldogs' as the 'Halls' displaced the 43XX moguls which in turn cascaded downwards, making many 'Bulldogs' surplus to requirements. The first 'Bulldog' was therefore withdrawn from service as early as 1929, 3320 *Avalon*, with two more, 3365 *Charles Grey Mott* and 3334 *Tavy*, in 1930. The frames of 3365 were then utilised to replace those of 'Duke' 3265 *Tre Pol and Pen* to create the prototype of the later 'Earl' or 'Dukedog' class. Six more were withdrawn in 1931 and seven in

3407 *Madras* storms over the summit at Patchway station on a winter's day with a Cardiff-Bristol train in the 1930s.
(GW Trust)

3421 (unnamed) on a Cheltenham-Swindon train at Foss Cross, 3 April 1921.
(GW Trust)

Unnamed 3437, built as 3727 in 1906, seen with an express on the North & West route, April 1925.
(I.C. Allan/GW Trust Collection)

3385 *Newport* with a down horsebox special train to Newbury for a race meeting, passing Twyford, c1920s. A Dean 4-wheel coach is at the back for the grooms.
(GW Trust)

3413 *James Mason* at Ashley Hill station, Bristol, c1920s.
(GW Trust)

3378 *Tiver Tawe* at Swansea on a stopping train for Carmarthen, c1920s. Note the train formed of former short wheelbase Metropolitan stock that was used for through trains to Moorgate.
(GW Trust)

3388, previously *Swansea*, but stripped of its name to avoid passenger confusion, with a Hereford-Paddington express entering Worcester Shrub Hill station past the loco shed, c1930.
(GW Trust)

3385 *Newport*, before being stripped of its name, with a semi-fast train for Oxford at Paddington, c1920s. A 'Saint' is in the adjacent platform. (GW Trust)

1932. However, other members of the class were still performing useful duties. In the West Country, although the 43XX and later 83XX replaced them in Cornwall and the 'Kings' and Castles' had displaced them on the longer distance trains east of Plymouth, they still acted as assistant engines over the South Devon banks, piloting expresses between Newton Abbot and Plymouth. A couple of recorded runs include a 1936 account of 3342 *Bonaventura* and an unidentified 'Castle' accelerating from a 48mph p-way slack at Tavistock Junction to hold 22mph on Hemerdon Bank with a load of 365 tons and touch an

3422 *Aberystwyth* at Bristol Temple Meads beside a 4575 'Small Prairie' 2-6-2T, 1929. (GW Trust)

3326 *Laira*, before it lost its name, on a Paddington-Oxford semi-fast service, in the late 1920s.
(Real Photos/J.M. Bentley Collection)

3330 *Orion* with the Kensington-West of England milk empties between Twyford and Sonning, in the late 1920s.
(Real Photos/J.M. Bentley Collection)

unusually high 68mph descending Rattery, passing through Totnes at 60mph and averaging 52mph on the climb to Dainton, topped at 30½mph. On another occasion on the up *Cornish Riviera* 3401 *Vancouver* assisted a 'King' as far as Hemerdon Box, reached in 12½ minutes start-to-stop, with a tare load of 370 tons.

In the early 1930s, nearly every GW depot had a 'Bulldog' or two for secondary duties, with Reading, Bristol, Swindon, Taunton, Laira and Hereford having a few more each. There were a few in South Wales at Cardiff and more in West Wales, especially at Neyland. And one at

3404 *Barbados* puts up a fine display hauling a motley collection of Dean four-wheelers and three horseboxes, in the West Midlands, in the mid-1920s.
(J.M. Bentley Collection)

Tondu for daily business travel from Porthcawl to Cardiff and Newport. Despite the steady withdrawals, the London, Wolverhampton and Worcester Divisions actually increased their allocations at this time. The increase in the London District was mainly based on the needs at Didcot after the Didcot-Newbury-Winchester line was raised to 'blue' level route availability. As scrapping continued, Newton Abbot increased its number of 'Bulldogs' in 1938, mainly for piloting work between Newton Abbot and Plymouth.

Also in 1936, O.S. Nock recorded personally a run on the 6.50pm

3334 *Tavy*, withdrawn from service in April 1930, passing West Drayton on an up Bristol-Paddington express in the 1920s. The long train is in the chocolate lake livery.
(J.M. Bentley Collection)

3383, unnamed, but previously called *Ilfracombe*, leaving Dawlish with the 4.30pm Paignton-Exeter stopping train, 2 September 1936.
(K Nunn/LGB Collection)

3398 *Montreal* passing Kensal Green with a Paddington-Oxford semi-fast service, August 1931.
(Photomatic/GW Trust Collection)

Chester to Wrexham behind 3373 *Sir William Henry* which held 33½mph on the four mile 1 in 82 climb of Gresford Bank with a load of 190 tons. The 12.1 miles were run in 18¾ minutes including a 10mph colliery subsidence slack near Wheatsheaf Junction. There are records too, although no timing logs of 'Bulldogs' on cross-country services between South Wales and Portsmouth and Bristol/South Wales and Birmingham, via the Cheltenham and Honeybourne route.

Between 1936 and 1939 withdrawn 'Bulldog' frames that were in good

3325, previously 3337 *Kenilworth*, here unnamed at Old Oak Common depot, c1930.
(J.M. Bentley Collection)

3341 *Blasius* passing Kensal Green with a down express, August 1931.
(Photomatic/J.M. Bentley Collection)

3353 *Pershore Plum*, previously named Plymouth, double-heading a 'Star' into Shrewsbury with a Paddington-Birkenhead express, c1930s.
(GW Trust)

THE BULLDOGS – OPERATION • 159

3446 *Goldfinch* with a Bristol-Westbury stopping train at Freshford station, 9 June 1930.

(H.C. Casserley/J M Bentley Collection)

3308, rebuilt 'Duke' 3280 *Falmouth*, now unnamed, on a freight train at Shrewsbury, c1935.

(Bob Miller Collection/MLS)

Rebuilt 'Duke' 3314 *Mersey* (previously 3322) with a freight at Stourbridge Junction, c1933.
(GW Trust)

3416 *John W Wilson* at Swanbridge on the Taunton-Barnstaple branch, c1935.
(GW Trust)

condition were matched with 'Duke' boilers to form the 'Dukedogs' which will be described in greater detail in Chapter 5. The withdrawn 'Bulldogs' used in this way were 3374/80/90/92, 3402-05/09-16/20/22-25/27-29/33/34/36/37/39.

The Railway Performance Society has just two logs, both in wartime conditions and over relatively short distance, neither in the West Country, both recorded by G.J. Aston. On 26 February 1941, 3396 *Natal Colony* had charge of the two-coach 8.47am Shepton Mallet-Bristol Temple Meads which stopped at all stations

Rebuilt 'Duke' 3309, previously 3283 *Maristow*, at Twyford on an up Oxford-Paddington semi-fast train, c1930.
(J.M. Bentley)

3377, previously named *Penzance*, arrives at Paddington with the 1.08pm local from Reading, c1938. Paddington Goods Shed is very prominent in the background.
(GW Trust)

Unnamed 3388, previously *Swansea*, on a local service near Mortimer on the Basingstoke-Reading line, c1936.
(GW Trust)

3393 *Australia* performs station pilot duties at Plymouth North Road, 8 May 1936.
(GW Trust)

to Yatton, and then ran over the twelve miles to Bristol in 21 minutes 52 seconds, including a dead stand for fifty seconds for signals at Flax Bourton and diversion to the slow lines at Parson Street. In between the 'Bulldog' was quite speedy, reaching 61mph at Nailsea and after the check, a rapid acceleration to 66mph just before the Parson Street slowing. The other run was with unnamed 3353 (formerly 3365 *Plymouth*) between Stourbridge Junction and Worcester Shrub Hill on 9 October 1941. No train details are given and only section times from Stourbridge Junction to Kidderminster (9mins 40secs),

3393 *Australia* departs Plymouth North Road with a lightweight Plymouth-Exeter stopping train, 8 May 1936. (M.Yarwood/GW Trust Collection)

3371 *Sir Massey Lopes* shunts stock at Yeovil Pen Mill, 21 May 1934. (GW Trust)

3341 *Blasius* at Eastleigh with a Reading-Portsmouth service formed with LSWR rolling stock, c1930s.
(GW Trust)

3410 *Columbia* near Shirley with a Birmingham-Stratford-Worcester express, 2 July 1936.
(GW Trust)

Kidderminster-Droitwich (12mins 23secs), Droitwich-Fernhill Heath (5mins 51secs) and finally Fernhill Heath-Worcester Shrub Hill (8mins 19secs).

D.S.M. Barrie, later General Manager of BR's Eastern Region, recorded another wartime run between Cardiff and Hereford with an immense 15-coach 465 ton gross train, hauled by 'Saint' 2949 *Stanford Court* that was given an assistant engine in the shape of locally allocated 'Bulldog' 3371 *Sir Massey Lopes* as far as Pontypool Road where one trailing parcels van was detached. Nothing over 60mph

3395 *Tasmania* leaves Dawlish station with an Exeter-Newton Abbot-Paignton stopping service, c1938. Note the gentleman in the foreground who seems more interested in the activity of the photographer than of the train.
(GW Trust)

3376 *River Plym* with a Swindon-Bristol stopping train near Bathampton, c1938.
(GW Trust)

3370 *Sir John Llewellyn* with a Didcot-Swindon local train near Steventon, c1935.
(GW Trust)

A 'Bulldog' thought to be 3330 but unnamed is seen at an unidentified location with an express in the mid-1930s.
(GW Trust)

3394 *Albany*, fitted with the Westinghouse brake and air-pump, at Wolverhampton Low Level on a southbound stopping service, c1933.
(GW Trust)

Rebuilt 'Duke' 3319, unnamed but formerly 3331 *Weymouth*, at Fratton, on a Portsmouth Town-Cardiff train, 5 August 1931.
(L. Hanson/J.M. Bentley Collection)

3353 *Pershore Plum* on a Birmingham-Stourbridge stopping service, at Birmingham Snow Hill, early 1930s.
(J.M. Bentley Collection)

3410 *Columbia* leaving Chester for Birkenhead with the down 'Zulu' in the early 1930s. Note the LNWR signals and the Dean large 0-4-2T on the right.
(Gordon Tidey/J.M. Bentley Collection)

3362 *Albert Brassey* at Crewe backing into one of the bay platforms for a service to Whitchurch and Wellington. A LNWR 'George V' 4-4-0 is in the background, c1920.
(Real Photos/J.M. Bentley Collection)

Unnamed 'Bulldog'
3426 double-heading LNW 'George V' class 5370 *Landrail* arriving at Chester from Manchester, with a train formed of LNWR rolling stock, c1930.
(Real Photos/J.M. Bentley Collection)

3395 *Tasmania* undergoing light repairs at Banbury shed, April 1932.
(GW Trust)

between Cardiff and Newport was recorded, and there were a series of signal checks before Newport station, but after leaving there three minutes late, the pair stormed through Caerleon at 53mph and sustained 48-45mph up most of the bank to Llantarnam Junction easing to 35mph at the top at Panteg Junction where the Eastern Valley line from Newport joined the North & West, just before the Pontypool Road stop. Arrival there was just three quarters of a minute late and the date was 1 July 1940.

At the end of the Second World War, fifty-three 'Bulldogs' remained in service with forty-five of them

3412 *John G Griffiths* with a Bristol-Plymouth semi-fast service near Westbury, 27 May 1935. Note the rear vehicle, an 'Ocean Mail' full brake parcels van.
(H.C. Casserley/J.M. Bentley Collection)

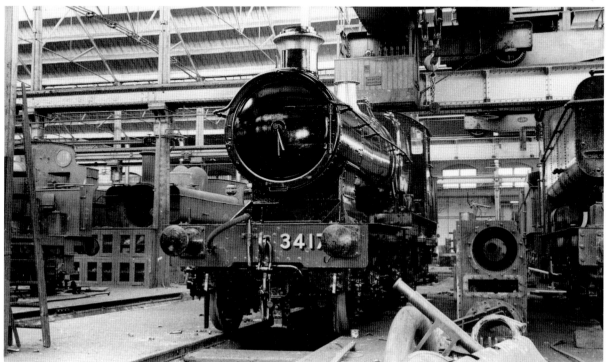

3417 *Lord Mildmay* of Fleet undergoing heavy repairs at Swindon Works B Shop, a class '1854' pannier tank behind, 18 October 1936.
(L. Hanson/J.M. Bentley Collection)

3363 *Alfred Baldwin* at Brent Knoll with a Weston-super-Mare-Taunton stopping train, 1938.
(GW Trust)

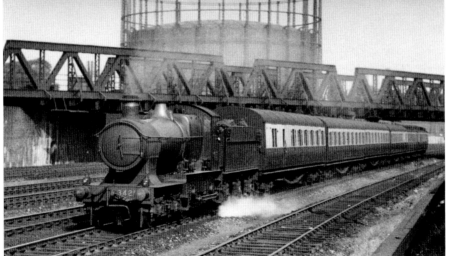

Unnamed 3421 passing Kensal Green on a Paddington-Oxford semi-fast service, c1938.
(GW Trust)

coming into BR ownership in 1948. The piloting of heavy expresses over the South Devon banks was one of their key remaining tasks. O.S. Nock photographed 3445 *Flamingo* at Penzance ready to double-head the up *Cornish Riviera* to Plymouth in the summer of 1947. A run over the South Devon banks on Christmas Eve 1948, when 3441 *Blackbird* piloted 6026 *King John* on a thirteen coach 460 ton train, recorded the Newton Abbot-Totnes section in 16 minutes 29 seconds start-to-stop, Totnes to Brent including the Rattery Incline in

17 minutes 19 seconds and on to Plymouth North Road in a further 28 minutes 59 seconds. Aller Junction was passed at 35mph and speed fell to 28mph at Stoneycombe and 17mph at Dainton summit. Starting from the Totnes stop, speed was only 19mph at Tigley Box, but had recovered to 30mph at Rattery. After Brent speed was in the low 50s for most of the way with a momentary 60mph down Hemerdon Bank. The run was recorded by P.W.B. Semmens and was published in the November 1989 *Railway Magazine*. O.S. Nock rode the footplate of a 'King' on the 11am Paddington which was piloted from Newton Abbot by

3442 *Bullfinch* with an up milk train at Birmingham Snow Hill, 1937. The tank chassis were owned by the GWR but the tanks by the dairies. A gas tank for the station domestic supplies is in the background.
(L. Hanson/J.M. Bentley Collection)

3442 *Bullfinch* at Swindon with a stopping train for Didcot, c1935.
(GW Trust)

3453 *Seagull* on the Taunton-Barnstaple line, c1938.

(M.M. South/GW Trust)

3452 *Penguin* pilots a Churchward 43XX mogul past Flax Bourton with a West of England-Birmingham holiday express, c1939.

(G.H. Soole/J.M. Bentley Collection)

3446 *Goldfinch,* and on another occasion in the up direction about the same time the *Cornish Riviera Limited* had 3391 *Dominion of Canada* assisting the 'King' on a fourteen coach train.

However, seventeen more 'Bulldogs' were withdrawn in 1948, with most of those remaining being the latest built, with the 'Birds' prominently among them. The last two survivors were 3453 *Seagull* and 3454 *Skylark* and the latter ran a railway enthusiasts' special train from Birmingham to

An unidentified 'Bulldog' progresses westwards near Dovey Junction with a stopping train, c1930.
(J.M. Bentley Collection)

3363 *Alfred Baldwin* at Bristol Temple Meads in the late 1930s.
(GW Trust)

3341 *Blasius* near Churston with a Kingswear-Paignton-Newton Abbot service in the immediate post-war period, c1947. (GW Trust)

Unnamed 3421 near the end of its life with a pick-up freight at Haddenham, c1947. An LNER Gresley brakevan is in the far yard. (GW Trust)

3363 *Alfred Baldwin* with an up freight approaches Gaer Junction Tunnel, Newport, 1946.
(J.G. Hubbard/John Hodge Collection)

3418 *Sir Arthur* Yorke (previously numbered 3708) near Reading with a freight, 1946. The freight train includes a Midland cattle wagon at the front, next an LNER cattle wagon and then a group of small 'Container A's loaded into wooden sided wagons instead of 'flats'.
(MLS Collection)

LEFT: 3335 unnamed, but formerly called *Tregothnan*, at Newton Abbot station, after assisting a train over the Devon banks from Plymouth, 31 August 1945. (H.C. Casserley/J.M. Bentley Collection)

ABOVE: 3408 *Bombay* at Didcot a year before its withdrawal, 29 March 1947. (HC Casserley/Author's Collection)

3375 *Sir Watkin Wynn* pilots an unidentified 'Castle' ready to leave Newton Abbot for Plymouth a few weeks before the 'Bulldog's' withdrawal, summer 1947. (GW Trust)

3400 *Winnipeg* and 'Star' 4028 swathed in leaking steam stand ready at Newton Abbot with a holiday train for Plymouth and Cornish resorts in the summer of 1948.
(J.M. Bentley Collection)

Swindon in June 1951, organised by the Stephenson Locomotive Society. 3454 seems to have been taken very gently with no more than 60mph under easy steam down Hatton Bank and after a series of checks, ran in the 54-58mph range from Banbury to Oxford with the light five coach load. On the return journey a little more energy was apparently displayed and 65mph was reached in a couple of places. However, both Reading-based locomotives did little work that year and were withdrawn in November.

3445 *Flamingo* at Plymouth North Road with the Churchward dynamometer car after use by one of the visiting engines in the 1948 locomotive exchange trials three months before 3445's demise, July 1948.
(J.M. Bentley Collection)

3454 *Skylark* on the SLS special train from Birmingham to Swindon, seen here between Didcot and Swindon, June 1951.
(GW Trust)

A **'Bulldog'** consigned to the scrapheap – 3386, built as 3448 *Paddington* in 1903, which was one of the few that survived under nationalisation, being withdrawn in November 1949, seen here after withdrawal on the Swindon 'dump' with pannier tank 2064, 8 October 1950.
(MLS Collection)

CHAPTER 4

THE '3521' CLASS
DESIGN & CONSTRUCTION

In January 1899, a 0-4-4 tank engine, built originally as a 0-4-2T in 1889 and changed to its revised wheelbase in 1891, emerged from Swindon Works in its third and dramatically different guise. Dean had built twenty standard gauge 0-4-2Ts, 3521-3540 in 1887, outside framed engines with a 17' 6" long wheelbase. A further batch of the 0-4-2 saddle tank engines, 3541-3559, were built in 1888-9 as broad gauge 'convertibles' for use in Cornwall, and 3560 was built as a side tank broad gauge 'convertible', but all in their original form were unstable and prone to derailment and an extra pair of wheels under the cab and bunker were provided to try to cure this problem. The saddle tank engines were particularly unstable and were rebuilt with side tanks. 3521 and 3548 had both derailed at Doublebois in 1895. However, with experience of the 'Dukes', Dean, by now very much guided by Churchward, decided to convert them to more useful engines, a 5' 2" wheeled 4-4-0 to augment the motive power available for secondary traffic on the heavily graded routes of the railway, and they were rebuilt between 1899 and 1902.

There were forty of these 0-4-4 tank engines, and the first to be rebuilt in this way was 3553 in January 1899. Twenty-six of them were built with domed boiler and flush round-topped firebox – the standard Swindon S2 boiler that was fitted to the '2301' class (Dean 'Goods'). Rebuilding involved the reversal of the positions of cylinders and firebox and would have required new inside frames. They retained the 5' 2" coupled

wheels of the tank engines, 17" x 24" cylinders and slide valves with Stephenson link motion. Total heating surface was 1,179sqft and the grate area 17.2sqft. For 3521-3540, boiler pressure was 160lbpsi, for 3541–3560 boiler pressure was 150lbpsi and the engine weight, 41 tons 4cwt, engine and tender 75 tons 9cwt. The bogies were of the same type fitted to the 4-2-2 and 4-4-0 express engines of the period but with 2' 8" diameter wheels

Standard gauge 0-4-4T 3554, converted from earlier 0-4-2Ts, c1895. Note the 'guivering' on the sides of the tank and bunker. The 'S' on the headlamp denotes that the engine is engaged on a shunting turn. Note also the Mansell wooden centred trailing wheels under the bunker.
(Bob Miller/MLS Collection)

A '3521' class 0-4-4T leaving Brent with a train for Plymouth, before rebuilding as a 4-4-0, c1895.
(GW Trust)

compared with 3' 8" on the 'Duke' bogies. They were attached to 2,000 gallon tenders of the type originally built for the 'Dukes', later fitted with 2,500 gallon capacity tenders. Tractive effort (85 per cent) was 14,263lb.

Some of the original boilers lasted until about 1907, but the pooling and swapping of boilers between the 4-4-0s meant that some of the '2301' boilers (S2) and the S4 with the large domes in a central position on the boiler barrel were exchanged. The eventual standard was the back dome Belpaire boiler fitted to 3546 in 1902 and 3544 in 1903. This boiler had a slightly increased heating surface (1,193sqft),

The derailment at Doublebois in 1895 involving 0-4-4Ts 3521 and 3548.
(GW Trust)

4-4-0 3546 as converted from 0-4-4T, with original round topped boiler, c1900.
(Bob Miller/MLS Collection)

3552 with round topped boiler, c1902.
(GW Trust)

3527 with round topped boiler, c1905.
(GW Trust)

3539 with Belpaire firebox, and short wheelbase tender, c1910.
(GW Trust)

a smaller grate area of 15.32sqft but higher boiler pressure of 180lbpsi (some were later pressed to 200lbpsi). The former tractive effort was increased to 17,120lb.

In June 1900, 0-4-4T 3528 was rebuilt using a 'Camel' type parallel domeless (D3) boiler and drumhead smokebox resting on a built-up saddle and the remaining fourteen tank engines still to be converted had boilers of this type. The total heating surface of these boilers was significantly increased to 1,561.65sqft and the grate area was an enlarged 21.35sqft. Boiler pressure was 180lbspsi. Otherwise, their dimensions were identical to the twenty-six locomotives already rebuilt, although because of the

Rebuilt 4-4-0 3543, with Belpaire firebox, c1910.
(MLS Collection)

3555 with Belpaire firebox at Birmingham, c1920.

(Bob Miller/MLS Collection)

The first 0-4-4T rebuilt as a 4-4-0 with a 'Camel' type parallel domeless boiler, 3528, at Plymouth North Road, c1902. Note the reversing lever inside the firebox cladding and the jack on the running plate.

(GW Trust)

3557 with Belpaire firebox, c1920.

(Bob Miller/MLS Collection)

boiler, the weight was increased by just under four tons. The locomotives rebuilt in this way were 3524/25/28/31-33/36/40/47/48/51/56/58/59. The last to be converted in October 1902 was 3532.

All fourteen engines received the later long coned boilers between 1907 and 1914 giving different dimensions – heating surface of 1,425.68sqft, grate area 20.35sqft, and increased boiler pressure of 195 or 200lbpsi, giving tractive effort of 18, 545 or 19,020lb. These engines and those with the 'Dean Goods' boilers were superheated from 1910 onwards although it was a gradual process with 3554 not receiving a superheated boiler until

3551 with parallel boiler at Plymouth Millbay depot, as rebuilt in 1900.
(GW Trust)

3524 with parallel boiler at Gloucester, 1910. Here the reversing lever has been 'hidden'.
(MLS Collection)

3558 with domeless parallel boiler at Bath, c1912.
(GW Trust)

3551 with taper long coned boiler shortly before withdrawal in 1929.
(MLS Collection)

1927, just three years before its withdrawal. In fact, five of the '2301' boilered engines were condemned before being superheated and three of the domeless boilered engines also. Eleven of the latter engines received domeless long-coned boilers with superheaters between 1910 and 1926, 3548 and 3551 just lasting a further three years in this condition before withdrawal in 1929. However, because of the standardisation and interchange of boilers between the

3528 with long cone tapered boiler at Reading shed, in front of an ROD 2-8-0, September 1925. (GW Trust)

4-4-0s, these boilers would have lived on, probably on 'Bulldogs'.

3541 was condemned in October 1913, presumably after extensive damage in a mishap, and the next withdrawals were of 3530 in 1922, 3560 in 1923 and 3522 in 1925. The remainder of the '2301' boilered engines were withdrawn in 1927, with just four lingering to the 1930s, 3557 outliving the others by several years to 1934. The domeless boilered engines lasted no longer, 3532 and 3558 being withdrawn as early as 1923, the rest going between 1926 and 1929, except for 3559 which was withdrawn in November 1931.

'Dean Goods' boilered 4-4-0 3529 shortly before withdrawal in 1927, paired with a short wheelbase tender. (GW Trust)

3542 with round topped boiler at Falmouth, with Dean gas-lit six-wheel coach in the centre, c1902. Note the 'baulk road' track.

(GW Trust)

OPERATION

About half of these locomotives were initially allocated to the West of England for branch line and secondary passenger and freight work, particularly to Launceston and Falmouth, although some were also sent to the Bristol Division, allocated to Bristol and Westbury. They had been displaced from the West of England by 1910 and transferred mainly to the Worcester Division, distributed between Gloucester, Worcester and Hereford sheds. One of the Dean boilered engines, 3555, was in the early 1920s,

a fixture on the 2.15pm Newport to Portishead all station passenger train, returning on the 5.30pm to Bristol Temple Meads, where it would pick up four vans of Wills tobacco for delivery in Cardiff.

In 1921, 3521 and 3546 were sold to the Cambrian Railway although they reverted to the GWR on the absorption of that railway shortly afterwards. However, other engines – 3542/44/45/54 – spent several years on the former Cambrian system at Oswestry, Machynlleth and Aberystwyth sheds. In the

Bristol and Gloucester areas, as in the West Country, they were superseded by both 'Bulldogs' and the varieties of 2-6-2 Prairie tanks, especially after the building of the '5101' class in 1929. This spelt their doom, although a few lingered on at Machynlleth, Kidderminster, Aberystwyth and Worcester.

Their mileage run since conversion as 4-4-0s varied from 626,000 for 3541 scrapped early in 1913, to 1,205,000 for 3557 – a very respectable figure given the type of limited work for which they were suitable.

3541 newly reboilered with Belpaire firebox
on a down express at Iver, c1905.
(GW Trust)

3545 with Belpaire firebox at Symonds Yat with the former Bristol & Exeter Railway inspection saloon, c1910.
(GW Trust)

3546 at Machynlleth, c1905. This locomotive and 3521 were later sold to the Cambrian Railway to replace the Cambrian 4-4-0s destroyed in the Abermule accident in 1921.
(Bob Miller/MLS Collection)

3558 shortly after rebuilding from an 0-4-4T to a 4-4-0 with a parallel domeless boiler, on a lightweight express at an unidentified location, but thought to be Taunton, c1902.
(GW Trust)

A '3521' class locomotive with Dean Goods boiler and Belpaire firebox alongside 'Bulldog' 3432 *River Yealm* at Truro, c1910.
(GW Trust)

Parallel boilered
3523 at Slough on a
stopping train to
Paddington, c1910.
(MLS Collection)

Parallel boilered 3528
on a horsebox special at
Bentley Heath, 1911.
(GW Trust)

Taper short cone boilered 3525 at Patchway
with a Cardiff-Bristol train, c1912.
(GW Trust)

Tapered long cone boilered 3547 on a Newton
Abbot-Exeter stopping train at Dawlish, c1920.
(MLS Collection)

Tapered long cone boilered 3559 enters Southampton Terminus station with a train from Reading, c1920. (GW Trust)

3555 with a local train to Stourbridge Junction at Birmingham Snow Hill, c1927. (GW Trust)

CHAPTER 5

THE DUKEDOGS
DESIGN & CONSTRUCTION

3265 *Tre Pol and Pen* at Reading depot, August 1924, before withdrawal and rebuilding with 'Bulldog' frames to form the prototype 'Dukedog' in January 1930.
(J.M. Bentley Collection)

With the building of Collett's mixed traffic locomotives, the 'Halls', 'Granges' and 'Manors' and the existing fleet of Churchward 2-6-0s, large numbers of the double-framed 4-4-0s became redundant and most of the Bulldogs and the 6' 8" coupled wheeled 'Badmintons', 'Atbaras' and 'Cities' were withdrawn from service between 1930 and 1935. The one group of locomotives to survive intact were the forty un-rebuilt 'Dukes', because of their light axle-load and 'yellow'

route availability, making them valued engines for routes such as the Didcot-Newbury-Winchester line and the former Cambrian lines in Central Wales. However, the 'Duke' frames were getting worn and many cracks were having to be patched.

One of the first 'Bulldogs' to be withdrawn from service was the 1903-built 3365 *Charles Grey Mott* (formerly 3417) at the end of 1929, and it was in Swindon Works at the same time as 'Duke' 3265 *Tre Pol and Pen*. 3265's frames were in bad condition and those of the condemned 3365 were in much better shape, so a

decision was made to retain the 'Duke' by replacing its curved frame with the straight frame of the 'Bulldog'. In this way, with the lighter boiler, the rebuilt 3265 retained its 'yellow' route classification. As locomotives are normally identified by their frame, this hybrid engine should have retained the 'Bulldog' identity number of 3365, but presumably to avoid ambiguity over this engine's route availability, it was still called a 'Duke' and kept its 3265 number. In its 'Duke' form it had run 918,405 miles and after reconstruction it ran a further 612,298 miles, giving a total of over 1.4m miles for the engine known as 3271/3265/9065 during its life, although its frame inherited from the 'Bulldog' ran a lesser mileage.

The cylinders, motion and cab of 3265 were retained as well as its boiler. The bogie wheels were a smaller diameter, 3' 2", possibly to ensure clearance with the new cylinder layout – the same as the double-framed passenger engines – the axleload over the coupled wheels was just under a ton heavier than the 'Duke' but over two tons lighter than a 'Bulldog', just enough for the civil engineer to accept it for the 'yellow' classified routes.

3365 *Charles Grey Mott* at Shrewsbury arriving on a stopping train off the Hereford line. This engine was withdrawn in December 1929 and its frames were used with the boiler, cab and motion of 'Duke' 3265 *Tre Pol and Pen* to be the prototype of the 'Dukedog' class, c1920s. The first vehicle is a LNW third class coach.
(GW Trust)

3265 *Tre Pol and Pen* after rebuilding to the 'Dukedog' form in 1930, but retaining its 'Duke' name and number at Banbury, 29 January 1939.
(W. Potter/MLS Collection)

3201 at Swindon Works after rebuilding from 'Duke' 3263 and 'Bulldog' 3412, March 1936. It retained its 'Duke' name, *St Michael*, at first, then was renamed *Earl of Dunraven*, then was unnamed when the name was applied to 'Castle' 5044. It was renumbered 9001 in 1946.

(GW Trust)

By 1935, several of the 'Dukes' had frames that were becoming uneconomic to repair – there was a limit on how many times they could be successfully patched. By then, a large number of the later 'Bulldogs' with straight frames were being withdrawn, so a decision was taken to follow the example of the successful conversion of 3265 and match the 'Bulldog' frames with the 'Duke' boiler, motion and cabs. Twenty of these rebuilt engines were constructed between March 1936 and June 1938 and at first it was proposed to retain the 'Duke' names,

the first rebuild, renumbered 3201 being turned out as *St Michael*, its 'Duke' ancestry being 3263 of that name. 3263 was matched with the frames of 3412 *John G Griffiths*. Any problems with the bogie clearance had been sorted out and the rebuilt engine retained the 3' 8" diameter bogie wheels of the 'Duke' class.

3200 followed in April 1936, the number originally being reserved for 3265 – which in fact was not renumbered until 1946, and then it stayed in the 'Duke' series rather than with the 'Dukedogs' as the rebuilt locomotives were eventually

nicknamed. A further eighteen were converted between 1936 and 1938 and were numbered 3202-3219 and initially all were named after Earls, many of whom were either associated with the GWR territory or had connections to the GW Board. Nameplates were fixed to 3200 and 3202-3212 with the new 'Earl' names and 3201 was renamed *Earl of Dunraven* instead of its original 'Duke' name, but before the nameplates could be fixed to the last series under construction (3213-3219) the names were switched to the latest batch of 'Castles' after, apparently, a

3202 *Earl of Dudley* at Swindon Works rebuilt from 'Duke' 3286 and 'Bulldog' 3416, immediately after construction in June 1936. (GW Trust)

3206 *Earl of Plymouth* shortly after construction using the parts from 'Duke' 3267 and 'Bulldog' 3428, at Didcot, 1937. (Bob Miller/MLS Collection)

number of the Earls objected to their names being allotted to such old-fashioned looking engines.

The names allocated and fixed were:

3200 *Earl of Mount Edgcumbe*
3201 *Earl of Dunraven*
3202 *Earl of Dudley*
3203 *Earl Cawdor*
3204 *Earl of Dartmouth*
3205 *Earl of Devon*
3206 *Earl of Plymouth*
3207 *Earl of St Germans*
3208 *Earl Bathurst*
3209 *Earl of Radnor*
3210 *Earl Cairns*
3211 *Earl of Ducie*
3212 *Earl of Eldon*

3211 *Earl of Ducie* on Aberystwyth shed alongside a sister 'Dukedog', 16 May 1937. (GW Trust)

3204, stripped of its *Earl of Dartmouth* nameplates, at Machynlleth shed, September 1938. (GW Trust)

3205, named *Earl of Devon*, at Aberystwyth station doubleheading a 'Dean Goods' 0-6-0, 3 August 1938.
(GW Trust)

Their names were removed in June and July 1937. The following names were allocated but the engines never received the names:

3213 *Earl of Powis*
3214 *Earl Waldegrave*
3215 *Earl of Clancarty*
3216 *Earl St. Aldwyn*
3217 *Earl of Berkeley*
3218 *Earl of Birkenhead*
3219 *Earl of Shaftesbury*

These names were transferred to 'Castles' newly constructed at Swindon, 5043-5062, replacing the 'Castle' names they had previously received.

3211, formerly named *Earl of Ducie*, undergoing its first Works overhaul at Swindon, 16 March 1939.
(GW Trust)

3217 after construction at Swindon Works, 13 March 1938. It was allocated the name *Earl of Berkeley* which was not carried until this locomotive was retained in preservation on the Bluebell Railway.
(GW Trust)

3219, allocated the name *Earl of Shaftesbury* which was never carried, on Swindon shed immediately after construction, alongside a Churchward 28XX 2-8-0, 1938.
(MLS Collection)

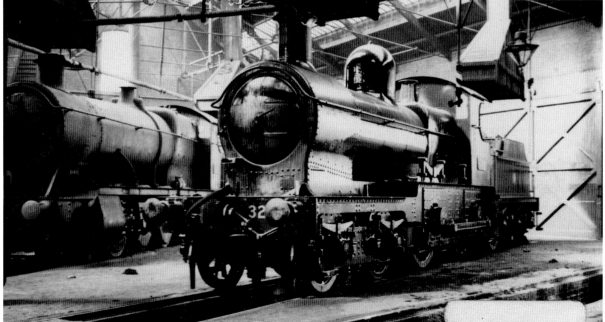

3215 allocated the name *Earl of Clancarty* which was used instead by 'Castle' 5058, at Didcot, 1 May 1938.
(MLS Collection)

3215 after its first Works overhaul, at Didcot, a class '2021' saddle tank behind, 5 February 1939.
(GW Trust)

3220 under construction in Swindon Works, using parts from 'Duke' 3279 and 'Bulldog' 3414, 13 November 1938.
(E. Smith/GW Trust Collection)

3216, works photo in the GW postwar plain green livery and GWR initials on the tender, just prior to the 1946 renumbering.
(Bob Miller/MLS Collection)

Officially classified as the 'Earl' class, the first twenty locomotives were complete by June 1938, and plans were made to convert the remaining 'Dukes' to this class. The latter group were to be fitted with new 'Duke' boilers designed for the possibility of 200lbpsi pressure although initially pressed at 180lb. Only nine locomotives, 3220-3228, had been completed when war broke out and the remaining eleven 'Dukes' were left to soldier on with their original 'Duke' frames.

Main dimensions of the rebuilt engines were: 18" x 26" cylinders,

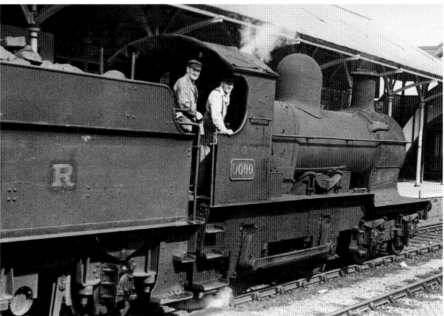

9000 at Welshpool, 24 August 1948.
(H C Casserley/GW Trust)

9001, formerly 3201 *St Michael/Earl of Dunraven*, at Oswestry in the mid-1950s.
(MLS Collection)

9017 at Machynlleth, c1949.
(MLS Collection)

9017 at Machynlleth again, but ten years later, 29 September 1959, a year before withdrawal and subsequent preservation.
(GW Trust)

bogie wheel diameter 3' 8", coupled wheels 5' 8", heating surface 1,192sqft, grate area 17sqft, engine weight 49 tons, total weight 89 tons, axleload over coupled wheels 15 tons 8cwt, tractive effort (85 per cent) 18,955 lb, tender capacity, 3,500 gallons. Some engines had 3,000 gallon water tenders reducing the total weight by just over three tons. In 1946 they were renumbered 9000-9028, retaining the last two digits of their previous number.

All the locomotives were taken at nationalisation into the stock of British Railways, and classified in the power category 2P, but three,

9022 at Oswestry shed, 1 May 1949.

(J.D. Darby/MLS Collection)

9015 at Reading shed, 1950.

(GW Trust)

9015 later in the mid-1950s. (GW Trust)

Swindon's 9018 at Bristol St Philip's Marsh, 29 July 1951. (GW Trust)

(9006, 9007 and 9019) were withdrawn in that year, 1948, without receiving smokebox numberplates. 9009 and 9014 were fully lined out in the BR mixed traffic livery in 1949, but the remainder of the class were painted plain black with the lion and wheel icon on the tender. 9001 and 9002 were withdrawn in 1954. Two more (9000 and 9003) went in 1955, but the rest lasted until 1957, with the last four, 9004, 9014, 9017 and 9018 remaining until 1960, 9014 and 9017 being withdrawn finally in October.

Swindon's 9011, also at Bristol St Philip's Marsh, 29 July 1951.
(GW Trust)

A three-quarters rear view of 'Dukedog' 9026, taken at Oswestry, with a pannier tank and a 'Manor', 29 July 1951.
(A.C. Gilbert/MLS Collection)

9027 at Aberystwyth with a couple of BR Standard 2MT 2-6-0s, 19 July 1953.
(MLS Collection)

9011, formerly 3211 *Earl of Ducie*, at Swindon shed, 25 April 1954.
(MLS Collection)

1938 built 9021, formerly 3221, at Machynlleth shed, 15 June 1958.
(MLS Collection)

9021 again, in the company of BR Standard 4-6-0 75020, at Aberystwyth shed, c1958.
(MLS Collection)

9015 and Collett 0-6-0 2264 on the scrap dump at Swindon, awaiting cutting up, 18 September 1960. 9015 had been withdrawn three months earlier.
(A.C. Gilbert/MLS Collection)

OPERATION

The prototype rebuilt 'Duke', 3265 *Tre Pol and Pen* was initially allocated to Didcot and was a frequent performer over the Didcot-Newbury-Winchester-Southampton line. It later moved to Machynlleth with many of the 'Dukedogs'.

Initially the new 'Earls' were allocated the duties of the 'Dukes' that they replaced. On completion of the twenty-nine locomotives in 1939,

they were distributed around the GWR system as follows:

Aberystwyth:	8
Oswestry:	7
Machynlleth:	3
Swindon:	3
Didcot:	2
Gloucester:	2
Tyseley:	2
Shrewsbury:	1
Stafford Road:	1

The eighteen allocated to the former Cambrian lines made up the bulk of their work, covering the Shrewsbury-Aberystwyth/Barmouth and Pwllheli route and the Ruabon-Bala-Barmouth line. The Shrewsbury engine would also have been used on these routes. The Swindon allocated three would have been used mainly on the former M&SWJR line from Cheltenham,

3265 *Tre Pol and Pen* at Kingsworthy with a Southampton-Didcot train, c1935.
(A.M. Russell/MLS Collection)

3265 *Tre Pol and Pen* leaving Barmouth with the 2.20pm Harlech to Birmingham Snow Hill, 29 August 1937.
(John Hodge Collection)

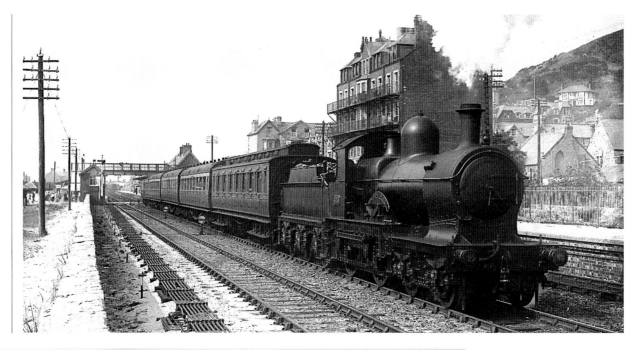

3201 *Earl of Dunraven* taking water at an unknown location with a holiday express, summer 1937.
(GW Trust)

through Swindon to Marlborough and Andover. The Didcot pair would have been occupied mainly on the line from there to Newbury and Winchester and the Gloucester pair would have worked on the Gloucester-Hereford route. Most of their work would have been on the local stopping passenger services, with some doubling up on the holiday traffic in the summer to the mid-Wales coastal resorts. After the Second World War and the strengthening of both the Didcot-Winchester / Southampton route and the Cambrian mainline, much of their work was taken over by the Churchward 43XX 2-6-0s and 'Manors' and so they found their way onto local freight work as well as the lightest local passenger services. During the winter months, many were put to store.

3208 *Earl Bathurst* leaving Crewe with a stopping service to Whitchurch and Wellington, c1937. 3208 would lose its nameplates that summer for transfer to 'Castle' 5051.
(GW Trust)

3212 *Earl of Eldon* leaving Bukeahead Woodside for Chester, with a train formed of LNWR rolling stock, May 1937.
(W. Potter/MLS Collection)

3202, formerly named *Earl of Dudley* climbing Talerddig bank with steam to spare, with a Machynlleth-Welshpool train, c1938.
(E.Smith/GW Trust)

3206, formerly *Earl of Plymouth*, at Eastleigh with a train from Didcot via Newbury and Winchester, 8 April 1939.
(GW Trust)

3206, a Didcot engine at that time, on the Didcot-Newbury-Winchester route, 22 July 1939. The leading vehicle is a short wheelbase Dean bogie coach.
(M. Yarwood/GW Trust)

3217 at Shrewsbury shortly after construction, with a semi-fast train for Welshpool and Aberystwyth, c1938.
(GW Trust)

3204, formerly *Earl of Dartmouth*, at Pwllheli with a stopping train for Barmouth and Machynlleth, c1937. (GW Trust)

3200, formerly named *Earl of Mount Edgcumbe* on arrival at Shrewsbury with a stopping train from Welshpool, c1937. (GW Trust)

The 'Dukedogs' were involved in only one train accident. In February 1947, 9023 was hauling the 8.45pm Cardiff – Avonmouth freight when it collided head-on with 6818 *Hardwick Grange* on the 9.20pm Avomouth – Salisbury freight on the single line between Hallen Marsh Junction and Pilning Low Level, after errors involving access to the single line by the 'Grange'. Both locomotives were badly damaged but were duly repaired at Swindon.

In 1950, the Cambrian engines were concentrated on Machynlleth shed which then had thirteen allocated for the Cambrian lines through Welshpool to Aberystwyth

3224 on a local train for Shrewsbury at Welshpool, c1945.
(GW Trust)

3219 on the Didcot-Winchester route, c1945. The first vehicle is a GW 'perishable' goods van.
(GW Trust)

3220 arrives at Portmadoc with a freight, 17 August 1946. (MLS Collection)

9026 on the 10.45am Machynlleth to Moat Lane and Welshpool, 28 July 1948. (H.C. Casserley/GW Trust)

9012 leaving Barmouth with a train for
Dovey Junction and Machynlleth, July 1948.
(A.C. Gilbert/MLS Collection)

9020 arrives at Machynlleth with a short pick-up goods train, 20 August 1948. (GW Trust)

9001 at Moat Lane on a freight, 28 July 1948. (H.C. Casserley/GW Trust)

and Pwllheli, and seven at Oswestry for the Ruabon-Barmouth route via Llangollen and Bala. The remaining engines were distributed:

Swindon:	3 (still for the M&SWJR)
Tyseley:	2
Didcot:	1

Three had already been withdrawn in 1948.

One of the Swindon engines, 9023, was sent to Newton Abbot in March 1954, and was tested on local services and piloting main line trains between Newton Abbot and Plymouth over the South Devon banks, but the experiment presumably was not successful

9005 stands at Aberdovey with a train for Machynlleth watched by a p-way gang waiting to place their Wickham trolley on the track, 20 July 1948.
(GW Trust)

9000 and 9027 doublehead a train for Welshpool and Shrewsbury out of Machynlleth, 20 August 1951. The train was over the load for a single 'Dukedog' on Talerddig bank.
(MLS Collection)

9002 stands in the sidings at Whitchurch while Churchward 2-6-0 5351 passes with a freight bound for Crewe, c1953.
(MLS Collection)

9005 runs light engine towards Barmouth having just crossed the Mawddach Estuary, 21 August 1951.
(N. Fields/MLS Collection)

9005 pilots 9028 (hidden from the camera) at Dovey Junction while a 45XX 2-6-2T waits to draw the Aberystwyth portion of the train back, 20 August 1951.
(MLS Collection)

9014, one of the last two survivors of the class, here seen ten years earlier at Criccieth, 20 September 1950.
(GW Trust)

9003 at Borth, 3 June 1952.
(GW Trust)

9004 at Ellesmere with a Crewe-Wellington train, 19 July 1954.
(GW Trust)

9021 runs into Ellesmere with a short Crewe-Wellington stopping train, whilst a 22XX 0-6-0 shunts in the yard, 26 June 1956.
(GW Trust)

9017 at Pencader working the 9.00am Aberystwyth-Carmarthen, passing a 58XX 0-4-2T, with a Churchward toplight 'concertina' coach, presumably having worked on the Newcastle Emlyn branch but here in the goods siding, 9 September 1952. (C.H.A. Townley/MLS Collection)

enough to have any engines
subsequently transferred for this
type of service.

As more 2-6-0s were drafted to
the Cambrian lines, the 'Dukedogs'
gradually lost most of their
remaining work and withdrawals
followed steadily between 1954 and
1960. The author came across a
number stored in the Swindon Stock
Shed along with a few 'Dean Goods'
and 4003 *Lode Star*, the latter
earmarked for preservation, during a
visit to Swindon Works in the
summer of 1956. In their final
summer season, while on holiday in
Barmouth, he spied a Birmingham-
Ruabon-Bala-Pwllheli train drawing

A West Wales
'Dukedog', 9010 at
Whitland with the
2.10pm to Carmarthen,
17 May 1954.
(K.P. Plant/MLS Collection)

One of the Swindon
based 'Dukedogs', 9011,
at Dunball with a
freight, c1955.
(MLS Collection)

9025 working hard near Portmadoc with a Pwllheli-Barmouth train, 15 July 1954.
(GW Trust)

9020 leaving Barmouth towards Towyn with a stopping train to Machynlleth, c1956.
(GW Trust)

9018 assists 7800 Torquay Manor with a heavy Aberystwyth-Manchester train, at Cemmaes Road, August 1956.
(E.Smith/GW Trust)

into Barmouth Junction headed by 9014 and 5399 whilst walking over Barmouth Bridge and raced to Barmouth station purchasing a ticket to Portmadoc to ride behind the pair, only to find that they were changed there for a pair of BR Standard 78000 2MT 2-6-0s!

Very little is recorded about their performance, most of their work being on light stopping trains which did not attract the attention of Britain's army of train timers in the 1950s and 60s. The Railway Performance Society has just one record in its archives, a run during the war of the first of the 1936 conversions. G.J. Aston recorded 3201 (formed of the frames of 3412

9022 and 2200 doublehead a freight at Welshpool, c1956.
(E.Smith/GW Trust)

One of the earliest specials, a Stephenson Locomotive Society (SLS) train with 9000, c1954.
(A.D.R. Williams/MLS Collection)

and the boiler and other parts from 3263 *St Michael*) on 26 April 1941 on a five coach local train from Ellesmere to Whitchurch, stopping at Welshampton and Bettisfield. Distances between stops were no more than three miles and 3201 attained 51mph and 47mph respectively between stations.

A much more interesting and detailed record of a 'Dukedog' can be found in O.S. Nock's book, *Four Thousand Miles on the Footplate* (Ian Allan, 1952) when 9027 (constructed from 'Bulldog' 3433 and 'Duke' 3280) had charge of the 1950 Summer Saturday 12.30pm Aberystwyth-Birmingham. Mr Nock joined the train at Machynlleth and

The two Swindon 'Dukedogs', 9023 and 9011 head an RCTS special train composed of Southern stock over the Thames at Battersea Reach en route for Swindon, 25 April 1954.
(GW Trust)

rode on the footplate to Welshpool where it was relieved by 7802 *Bradley Manor*. The 'Dukedog' had a reasonable load, seven coaches, 221 tons tare, 235 gross, and for the long 1 in 52 climb to Talerddig summit, an assisting engine in the form of small prairie tank 4581 was provided. (The load limit for the 'Duke' class and presumably the 'Dukedogs' also was 182 tons eastbound. A pair of 'Dukedogs' or 'Dukedog' and an assistant engine were permitted to take 360 tons.) The train, after attaching the pilot, left nine minutes late and the run initially was plagued with signal checks from

9023 and 9011 on arrival at Swindon with the RCTS rail enthusiasts' special, 25 April 1954. (GW Trust)

9017 with a rail enthusiasts' special train from Brecon at Newport, alongside pannier tank 3714, c1957. (MLS Collection)

9015 heads the Farnborough Railway Enthusiasts' Club *South Midlander* special at Ettingen in Warwickshire, 24 April 1957.
(GW Trust)

another 90XX-hauled stopping train ahead which itself was being delayed crossing down trains off the crowded single line. From the Llanbrynmair signal stand, the pair of engines accelerated to 30mph and then held 28-29mph on the climb before a stop at the top of the bank to release the pilot. 9027's driver used 35 per cent cut-off and regulator well into the second valve, eased to 32 per cent near the summit. Despite the checks Talerddig was reached nearly seven minutes under schedule (although two minutes late) and with yet

another signal stand at Carno, arrival at Moat Lane Junction was only 1½ minutes late, after a 60mph dash through Pontdolgoch. The train left on time and arrived early at Newtown, attaining 54½mph, but was delayed there for over four minutes awaiting a down train. The final 13.7 mile leg on to Welshpool took 21 minutes 30 seconds with a p-way slack to 15mph before Forden. A final spurt to 65mph after that and arrival at Welshpool was just a minute late having regained three and a half minutes of lost time on this section. Nock reported that

9027 was 'in splendid nick, steaming well and riding very smoothly'. On the near forty mile run, 9027 had used just 1,400 gallons of water, 36 to the mile, economical for the heavily graded terrain and the stopping and starting from stations and checks.

Many special enthusiast trains used the remaining 'Dukedogs' as requested power in the last years of their lives, with the two Swindon engines, 9011 and 9023, and the last two Machynlleth 'Dukedogs', 9014 and 9017, the latter destined for preservation.

Two 'Dukedogs', 9017 and 9014, head the annual Talyllyn AGM Special train from London to Towyn over the Cambrian section of the route, 26 September 1959.
(GW Trust)

9017 pilots Churchward mogul 6300 out of Shrewsbury on the annual Talyllyn AGM special, believed to be in May 1960.
(GW Trust)

PRESERVATION

9017 was one of the last two survivors. It was built in March 1938 at a cost of £2,398, plus £834 for a reconditioned tender from a 43XX mogul, using the frames of 1906 built 'Bulldog' 3425 (unnamed) and according to Swindon records, boiler, motion and cab from 1895 built 3258 *The Lizard*. A very helpful communication from Fred Bailey, one of the Bluebell Railway volunteers working with Keith Sturt, the Bluebell Workshop Manager during the renovation of 3217, advised me that he noted the origin of following parts:

- Frames from Bulldog 3425 as indicated in the Swindon records
- Cab & cab windows from 3258 *The Lizard,* as per Swindon records
- Driving axlebox from Aberdare 2-6-0 2620
- Lifting links from Duke 3289 (initially named *St Austell* later unnamed)
- Boiler – it was recorded as initially fitted in 1938 with boiler number 3277 which was originally fitted to Duke 3277 *Earl of Devon* (later 3270), but the current boiler is number 3205 built new in 1935 and fitted to 9017 in October 1955 at Stafford Road Works.

Inspection of many GW engines in later years revealed parts of the motion inscribed with two or three former numbers and it is clear that during regular overhauls, standard parts were removed, machined and returned to different engines. It is possible that the accountants for purely book-keeping purposes recorded 3217 with 3258's parts, when the reality was that the parts were from other locomotives including 3282, a number also found on parts of the motion, in which case it throws into doubt most of the accepted identities of the locomotives that formed the 'Dukedogs'.

3217 was superheated in 1910 and, as 9017, was still at work on the Cambrian section, operating out of Machynlleth until its withdrawal in October 1960. It had run 422,597 miles as a 'Dukedog' between 1938 and 1960.

It survives in preservation at the Bluebell Railway. Numbered originally as 3217 and allocated the name *Duke of Berkeley* which was never carried but fixed to 'Castle' 5060 instead, it arrived there on 15 February 1962, purchased by a private individual, T.R. Gomm of Birmingham. It acquired the nameplates from 5060 when that engine was withdrawn in 1963 and carried the post war numberplates of 9017 until the withdrawal of Collett 0-6-0 3217 in 1965, when those were acquired for use on the preserved 'Dukedog' when it was repainted in GWR green livery and its nameplates fitted. It was taken out of operation on the heritage railway in 1973 and returned after a lengthy storage to be overhauled in 1980, returning to traffic in 1982. Its last major overhaul, involving fitting a new smokebox tubeplate and new sections of both the front and back main frames, was in October 2003 when its private owner donated it to the Bluebell Railway on condition that it remained in service on that line.

It was repainted in BR black livery in April 2009, retaining its nameplates, both those and the numberplates having a red background as was sometimes the case in the 1950s for ex GW mixed traffic locomotives. It made a visit to the Llangollen Railway in 2009, where it had been in BR service. After a series of boiler and mechanical failures in June 2011, it remains on static display at Sheffield Park awaiting its next major overhaul.

APPENDIX –
DIMENSIONS, WEIGHT DIAGRAMS & STATISTICS

Duke class

Dimensions

Cylinders:	18" diameter x 26" stroke
Coupled wheels:	5' 7½" diameter
Bogie wheels:	3' 7½" diameter
Boiler pressure:	160lbpsi
Heating surface:	1,400.85sqft
Grate area:	19.11sqft
Axle-weight:	15.35 tons maximum
Weight, engine:	46 tons
Weight, tender:	24 tons
Total weight:	70 tons
Tractive effort (85%):	16,848lb

Dimensions
(with Belpaire firebox)
As above, except:

Boiler pressure:	180lbpsi
Heating surface:	1,289.85sqft
Grate area:	18.37sqft
Tractive effort (85%):	18,970lb

Weight Diagrams

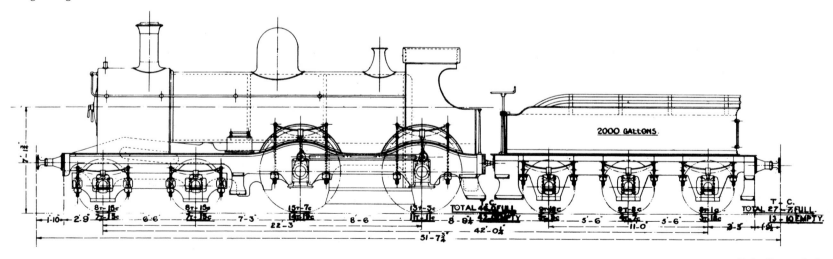

Duke Class as built

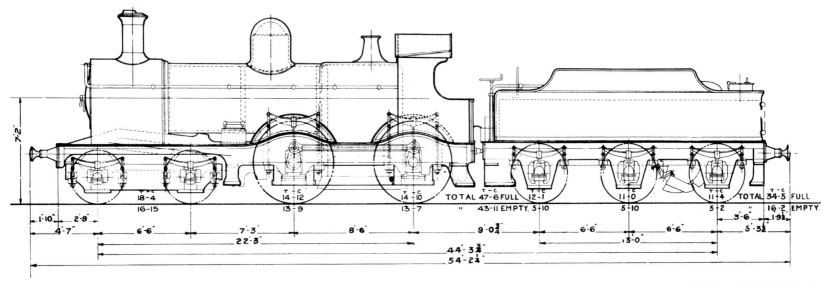

Duke Class with Belpaire boiler

Statistics

Twenty Dukes were rebuilt with taper boilers between 1902 and 1909, renumbered 3300-3319 and their last depot before rebuilding and their final mileage as a Duke is given below. Their statistics as Bulldogs are given in the next section of the appendix. The South Devon allocation in 1895 was either Plymouth Millbay or Newton Abbot.

No.	Name	Built	1st depot	1912 No.	1946 No.	Last depot	Withdrawn	Mileage
3252	*Earl of Cornwall*	5/95	S.Devon	3252		Aberystwyth	8/37*	1,054,247
3253	*Pendennis Castle+*	5/95	Plymouth	3300		Neyland	11/08**	462,175
3254	*Boscawen*	7/95	S.Devon	3253		Welshpool	1/39*	1,178,092
3255	*Cornubia*	7/95	S.Devon	3254	9054	Portmadoc	6/50	1,632,815
3256	*Excalibur*	8/95	S.Devon	3255		Aberystwyth	5/36*	1,106,003
3257	*Guinevere*	8/95	Paddington	3256		Didcot	8/39*	1,327,191
3258	*King Arthur+*	8/95	S.Devon	3257		Machynlleth	5/37*	1,123,478
3259	*The Lizard*	9/95	S.Devon	3258		Tyseley	12/37*	1,235,210
3260	*Merlin*	9/95	S.Devon	3259		Machynlleth	10/38*	1,193,623
3261	*Mount Edgcumbe*	9/95	S.Devon	3260		Gloucester	4/38*	1,211,328
3262	*Powderham+*	4/96	Paddington	3301		Paddington	10/06**	453,343
3263	*Sir Launcelot*	4/96	Paddington	3302		W'hampton	7/07**	377,102
3264	*St Anthony+*	5/96	Swindon	3303		Bordesley Jn	12/07**	347,597
3265	*St Germans+*	5/96	S.Devon	3261		Gloucester	2/37*	1,131,444
3266	*St Ives+*	5/96	Plymouth	3262		Pwllheli	3/36*	1,114,275
3267	*St Michael*	6/96	Exeter	3263		Oswestry	3/36*	1,243,901
3268	*River Tamar*	6/96	Exeter	3304		Bristol	6/06**	401,357
3269	*Tintagel+*	6/96	N. Abbot	3305		Plymouth	5/07**	416,261
3270	*Trevithick*	6/96	N'ton Abbot	3264	9064	Gloucester	12/49	1,373,804
3271	*Tre Pol and Pen*	7/96	Plymouth	3265		Tyseley	1/30***	918,405

No.	Name	Built	1st depot	1912 No.	1946 No.	Last depot	Withdrawn	Mileage
3272	*Amyas*	8/96	N'ton Abbot	3266		Didcot	1/38*	1,049,388
3273	*Armorel*	11/96	Paddington	3306		Paddington	2/02**	191,757
3274	*Cornishman*	11/96	N.Abbot	3267		Didcot	11/36*	1,152,697
3275	*Chough*	11/96	N.Abbot	3268		Oswestry	3/39*	1,235,312
3276	*Dartmoor*	12/96	Paddington	3269		Oswestry	9/36*	1,098,194
3277	*Earl of Devon+*	1/97	N.Abbot	3270		Pwllheli	4/39*	1,255,781
3278	*Eddystone*	1/97	Weymouth	3271		Aberystwyth	5/36*	1,067,596
3279	*Exmoor*	1/97	Paddington	3307		Hereford	12/07**	372,819
3280	*Falmouth+*	1/97	Plymouth	3308		Carmarthen	1/09**	431,875
3281	*Fowey+*	1/97	Paddington	3272	9072	Aberystwyth	6/49	1,280,999
3282	*Maristow*	2/97	Weymouth	3309		Exeter	7/07**	318,411
3283	*Mounts Bay*	2/97	Weymouth	3273	9073	Shrewsbury	12/49	1,298,626
3284	*Newquay+*	2/97	Plymouth	3274		Tyseley	11/36*	1,115,589
3285	*St Erth+*	2/97	Unknown	3275		Oswestry	5/36*	1,077,901
3286	*St Just+*	2/97	Paddington	3310		Cardiff	9/08**	391,450
3287	*St Agnes+*	3/97	Exeter	3276	9076	Shrewsbury	11/49	1,316,344
3288	*Isle of Tresco*	3/97	N.Abbot	3277		Aberystwyth	1/37*	1,073,501
3289	*Trefusis*	3/97	N.Abbot	3278		Swindon	1/39*	1,048,317
3290	*Tor Bay*	3/97	Swindon	3279		Swindon	8/38*	1,065,803
3291	*Tregenna+*	3/97	Swindon	3280		Swindon	5/39*	1,288,037
3312	*Bulldog*	10/98	Swindon	3311		Swindon	3/06**	218,818
3313	*Cotswold*	3/99	Swindon	3281		Tyseley	2/37*	1,080,691
3314	*Chepstow Castle+*	3/99	Plymouth	3282		Didcot	10/37*	1,024,501
3315	*Comet*	3/99	Penzance	3283	9083	Didcot	12/50	1,219,486
3316	*Isle of Jersey*	4/99	Salisbury	3284	9084	Oswestry	4/51	1,393,161
3317	*Katerfelto*	4/99	Plymouth	3285		Gloucester	1/37*	963,845
3318	*Isle of Guernsey*	3/99	Salisbury	3312		Swindon	2/08**	315,915
3319	*Jupiter*	4/99	Plymouth	3313		Landore	2/08**	276,585
3320	*Meteor*	4/99	Swindon	3286		Reading	4/36*	1,060,529
3321	*Mercury*	4/99	N.Abbot	3287	9087	Aberystwyth	7/49	1,163,998
3322	*Mersey*	4/99	Stafford Rd	3314		Neath	11/07**	283,031
3323	*Mendip*	6/99	Paddington	3288		Aberystwyth	4/36*	1,114,305
3324	*Quantock*	6/99	Paddington	3315		Swindon	12/08**	311,238
3325	*St Columb+*	6/99	Penzance	3316		Swindon	12/08**	323,122
3326	*St Austell+*	7/99	Plymouth	3289	9089	Oswestry	7/51	1,187,215
3327	*Somerset*	7/99	Plymouth	3317		OOC	5/08**	317,368
3328	*Severn*	7/99	Plymouth	3290		Oswestry	1/39*	1,134,913
3329	*Thames*	7/99	Plymouth	3291	9091	Welshpool	2/49	1,250,960
3330	*Vulcan*	7/99	Plymouth	3318		Exeter	12/08**	281,974
3331	*Weymouth+*	8/99	Plymouth	3319		Cardiff	7/07**	281,000

   * rebuilt with 'Bulldog' frames as 'Dukedog'

  ** rebuilt with taper boiler as a 'Bulldog'

*** rebuilt in 1930 with 'Bulldog' frames as a prototype 'Dukedog' but retaining 'Duke' identity, withdrawn from Oswestry depot in December 1949, final mileage 1,476,550

  + name removed as used on later GW locomotives or to avoid passenger confusion

Bulldog class

Dimensions (as for 3352 'Camel' standard class with parallel domeless boiler)

Cylinders:	18" diameter x 26" stroke
Coupled wheels:	5' 8" diameter
Bogie wheels:	3' 8" diameter
Boiler pressure:	180lbpsi
Heating surface:	1,663.02sqft
Grate area:	21.45sqft
Axle-weight:	17 tons 12cwt
Weight, engine:	51 tons 16cwt
Weight, tender:	33 tons or 40 tons
Total weight:	84 tons 16cwt or 91 tons 16cwt
Tender capacity:	3,000 gallons, 4 tons coal, or 3,500 gallons, 6 tons coal

Dimensions (as with No.2 standard boiler)

As above, except:	
Boiler pressure:	195lbpsi, later 200bpsi
Heating surface:	1,396.58sqft
Grate area:	20.35sqft
Tractive effort (85%):	21,000 lb

Dimensions (as with No.4 standard boiler)

As above, except:	
Boiler pressure:	200lbspsi
Heating surface:	1,818,12sqft
Grate area:	20.56sqft
Tractive effort (85%):	21,000lb

Weight diagrams

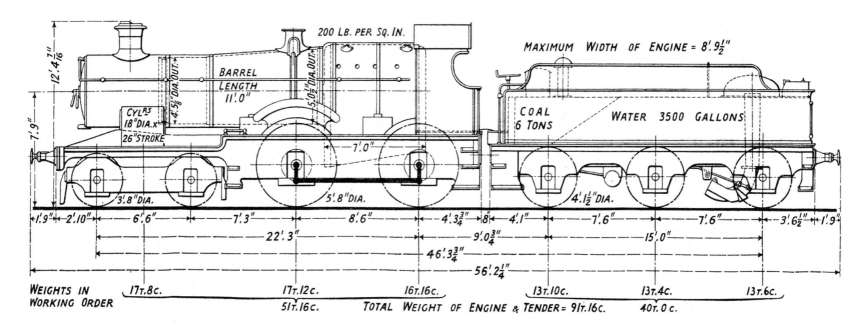

Bulldog Class

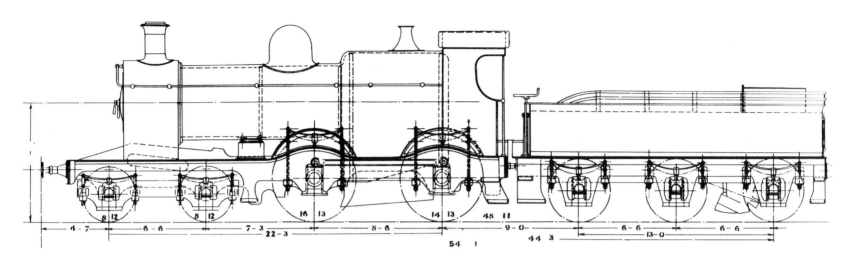

3312 as built

Statistics

The first depot shown for those engines numbered 3300 – 3319 (Dukes rebuilt as Bulldogs) is their first depot after rebuilding.
For actual first depot see listed as Dukes in previous section.

No.	Name	Built	1st depot	1912 No.	Last depot	Withdrawn	Mileage
3253	*Pendennis Castle**	5/95-11/08	Plymouth	3300	Bristol Bath Rd	2/36	1,337,808
3262	*Powderham**	4/96-10/06	OOC	3301	Worcester	5/31	1,246,946
3263	*Sir Launcelot*	4/96-7/07	Neath	3302	Old Oak Common	7/32	1,014,769
3264	*St Anthony**	5/96-12/07	Tyseley	3303	Gloucester	5/32	1,091,799
3268	*River Tamar*	6/96-6/07	P'pool Rd	3304	Reading	11/34	1,172,128
3269	*Tintagel**	6/96-5/07	Taunton	3305	Swindon	9/36	1,262,884
3273	*Armorel*	11/96-2/02	Cardiff	3306	Swindon	1/39	1,285,021
3279	*Exmoor*	1/97-12/07	Chester	3307	Hereford	5/33	1,126,682
3280	*Falmouth**	1/97-1/09	Landore	3308	Bristol Bath Rd	8/36	1,221,138
3282	*Maristow*	2/97-9/08	Plymouth	3309	Crewe	5/34	1,173,136
3286	*St Just**	2/97-9/08	N.Abbot	3310	Carmarthen	5/32	1,046,735
3312	*Bulldog*	10/98-3/06	Swindon	3311	Pontypool Rd	4/32	1,067,519
3316	*Guernsey#*	3/99-2/08	Swindon	3312	Bristol Bath Rd	4/31	1,027,336
3318	*Jupiter*	4/99-2/08	OOC	3313	Newton Abbot	4/46	1,332,919
3322	*Mersey*	4/99-11/07	Neath	3314	Gloucester	11/34	984,018
3324	*Quantock*	6/99-12/08	Swindon	3315	Worcester	7/31	987,371
3325	*St Columb**	6/99-12/08	Penzance	3316	Hereford	4/38	1,194,184
3327	*Somerset*	7/99-5/08	OOC	3317	Bristol Bath Rd	4/31	996,145
3330	*Vulcan*	7/99-12/08	Plymouth	3318	Hereford	2/34	1,037,778
3331	*Weymouth**	8/99-7/07	Weymouth	3319	Reading	5/32	1,113,803
3332	*Avalon*	11/99	Exeter	3320	Hereford	6/29	996,475
3333	*Brasenose*	11/99	Exeter	3321	Tyseley	3/35	1,184,162
3334	*Eclipse*	11/99	Weymouth	3322	Gloucester	3/35	983,166
3335	*Etona*	11/99	Weymouth	3323	Reading	8/35	1,060,355

No.	Name	Built	1st depot	1912 No.	Last depot	Withdrawn	Mileage
3336	*Glastonbury**	12/99	Weymouth	3324	Didcot	6/35	1,061,388
3337	*Kenilworth**	12/99	Weymouth	3325	Oxford	9/35	1,093,374
3338	*Laira**	1/00	Cardiff	3326	Old Oak Common	11/33	1,043,892
3339	*Marco Polo*	1/00	Oxford	3327	Chester	3/36	1,065,318
3340	*Marazion**	1/00	Oxford	3328	Hereford	4/34	1,055,620
3341	*Mars*	1/00	Paddington	3329	Salisbury	5/32	972,424
3342	*Orion*	2/00	Shrewsbury	3330	Bristol SPM	8/38	1,121,099
3343	*Pegasus*	2/00	Paddington	3331	Taunton	2/34	1,084,772
3344	*Pluto*	2/00	Stafford Rd	3332	Landore	9/31	884,472
3345	*Perseus*	2/00	Oxford	3333	Hereford	9/32	935,683
3346	*Tavy*	2/00	Weymouth	3334	Gloucester	3/30	961,940
3347	*Tregothnan**	2/00	Plymouth	3335	Exeter	10/48	1,397,566
3348	*Titan*	3/00	Plymouth	3336	Newton Abbot	12/35	1,026,606
3349	*The Wolf*	3/00	Plymouth	3337	Hereford	5/34	1,023,356
3350	*Swift*	3/00	Truro	3338	Chester	11/33	972,409
3351	*Sedgemoor*	3/00	Plymouth	3339	Worcester	6/34	1,052,826
3352	*Camel*	10/99	Swindon	3340	Swindon	5/34	?
3353	*Blasius*	5/00	Plymouth	3341	Exeter	11/49	1,364,467
3354	*Bonaventura*	6/00	N.Abbot	3342	Chester	10/38	1,195,206
3355	*Camelot*	6/00	Exeter	3343	Westbury	4/34	992,234
3356	*Dartmouth**	6/00	Plymouth	3344	Carmarthen	1/34	933,494
3357	*Exeter#*	6/00	Plymouth	3345	Weymouth	12/35	1,170,839
3358	*Godolphin*	10/00	Oxford	3346	Westbury	1/34	992,077
3359	*Kingsbridge**	10/00	N.Abbot	3347	Hereford	8/36	1,101,637
3360	*Launceston**	10/00	N.Abbot	3348	Worcester	11/34	1,053,646
3361	*Lyonesse*	10/00	Exeter	3349	Hereford	11/34	1,091,964
3362	*Newlyn**	11/00	N.Abbot	3350	Hereford	7/35	1,141,882
3353	*One and All*	11/00	Plymouth	3351	Worcester	4/31	1,018,515
3364	*Pendragon*	11/00	Swindon	3352	Shrewsbury	11/33	1,029,285
3365	*Plymouth*#*	11/00	N.Abbot	3353	Worcester	12/46	1,462,251
3366	*Restormel**	11/00	Swindon	3354	Westbury	11/34	1,082,972
3367	*St Aubyn**	11/00	Paddington	3355	Hereford	1/34	1,073,595
3368	*Sir Stafford*	11/00	Stafford Rd	3356	Reading	1/36	1,084,272
3369	*Trelawney*	11/00	Gloucester	3357	Exeter	11/34	993,770
3370	*Tremayne*	12/00	Gloucester	3358	Crewe	11/45	1,347,587
3371	*Tregeagle*	12/00	Bristol	3359	Chester	7/36	1,109,635
3372	*Torquay**	12/00	N.Abbot	3360	Tyseley	11/34	1,091,737
3413	*Edward VII**	12/02	Didcot	3361	Taunton	9/47	1,427,610
3414	*Albert Brassey*	12/02	Shrewsbury	3362	Hereford	4/37	1,095,977
3415	*Baldwin#*	1/03	Carmarthen	3363	Westbury	10/49	1,296,221
3416	*Bibby#*	2/03	Plymouth	3364	Westbury	6/49	1,188,658
3417	*C G Mott#*	2/03	Didcot	3365	Hereford	12.29+	864,252
3418	*Earl of Cork*	2/03	Weymouth	3366	Chester	4/48	1,225,527
3419	*Evan Llewellyn*	2/03	Bristol	3367	Bristol SPM	9/35	1,025,252
3420	*Ernest Palmer#*	2/03	Cardiff	3368	Worcester	4/35	1,027,982
3421	*MacIvor#*	2/03	Swindon	3369	Tyseley	7/36	876,921
3422	*Sir John Llewellyn*	3/03	Neyland	3370	Bristol Bath Rd	1/39	1,187,312

No.	Name	Built	1st depot	1912 No.	Last depot	Withdrawn	Mileage
3423	*Sir Massey#*	3/03	Plymouth	3371	Westbury	11/44	1,255,525
3424	*Sir Nigel#*	3/03	Swindon	3372	Hereford	11/36	1,026,925
3425	*Sir W H Wills#*	5/03	Paddington	3373	Tyseley	2/39	1,185,525
3426	*Walter Long*	5/03	Paddington	3374	Exeter	6/37	1,029,907
3427	*Sir Watkin Wynn*	5/03	Paddington	3375	Newton Abbot	9/47	1,203,510
3428	*River Plym*	5/03	Plymouth	3376	Didcot	9/48	1,255,072
3429	*Penzance**	5/03	Plymouth	3377	Worcester	3/51	1,343,891
3430	*River Tawe**	5/03	Landore	3378	Swindon	11/45	1,192,738
3431	*River Fal*	5/03	Truro	3379	Gloucester	6/48	1,267,268
3432	*River Yealm*	5/03	Exeter	3380	Bristol Bath Rd	12/37	1,134,703
3443	*Birkenhead**	9/03	Plymouth	3381	Wellington	11/35	942,701
3444	*Cardiff**	9/03	Plymouth	3382	Worcester	11/49	1,222,882
3445	*Ilfracombe**	9/03	Exeter	3383	Newton Abbot	12/49	1,348,274
3446	*Liverpool**	10/03	Chester	3384	Swindon	5/36	1,036,151
3447	*Newport**	10/03	Cardiff	3385	Didcot	11/34	1,081,343
3448	*Paddington**	9/03	Plymouth	3386	Reading	11/49	1,258,126
3449	*Reading**	10/03	Plymouth	3387	Banbury	11/34	884,020
3450	*Swansea**	10/03	Plymouth	3388	Hereford	10/35	1,097,096
3451	*Taunton**	10/03	Plymouth	3389	Hereford	11/45	1,216,372
3452	*Wolverhampton**	10/03	Plymouth	3390	Carmarthen	3/39	1,023,517
3453	*Dominion of Canada*	1/04	Chester	3391	Plymouth Laira	5/49	1,202,804
3454	*New Zealand*	1/04	Chester	3392	Cardiff	1/37	961,370
3455	*Australia*	1/04	Plymouth	3393	Worcester	11/49	1,253,002
3456	*Albany*	1/04	Plymouth	3394	Worcester	11/34	893,250
3457	*Tasmania*	1/04	N.Abbot	3395	Exeter	9/48	1,162,641
3458	*Natal Colony*	1/04	Neyland	3396	Didcot	2/48	1,272,841
3459	*Toronto*	2/04	Swindon	3397	Neyland	11/34	882,271
3460	*Montreal*	2/04	Neyland	3398	Plymouth Laira	9/35	951,662
3461	*Ottawa*	2/04	Cardiff	3399	Chester	10/47	1,263,616
3462	*Winnipeg*	2/04	Cardiff	3400	Exeter	5/49	1,209,463
3463	*Vancouver*	3/04	Plymouth	3401	Hereford	11/49	1,231,451
3464	*Jamaica*	3/04	Neyland	3402	Herefor	1/37	976,828
3465	*Trinidad*	3/04	Neyland	3403	Croes Newydd	1/37	994,190
3466	*Barbados*	3/04	Weymouth	3404	Oxford	9/37	941,690
3467	*Empire of India*	3/04	N.Abbot	3405	Crewe	4/37	1,061,213
3468	*Calcutta*	3/04	N.Abbot	3406	Hereford	11/49	1,218,509
3469	*Madras*	4/04	Neyland	3407	Newton Abbot	12/49	1,194,665
3470	*Bombay*	4/04	Exeter	3408	Didcot	4/48	1,271,326
3471	*Queensland*	4/04	Neyland	3409	Hereford	2/39	1,145,146
3472	*Columbia*	4/04	Cardiff	3410	Tyseley	11/36	958,448
3701	*Baldwin#*	4/06	Bristol	3411	Cardiff	10/38	979,071
3702	*John G Griffiths*	4/06	Taunton	3412	Bristol Bath Rd	3/36	882,079
3703	*James Mason*	4/06	Neyland	3413	Westbury	8/36	916,104
3704	*A H Mills#*	5/06	Taunton	3414	Crewe	10/38	893,629
3705	*George A Wills*	5/06	Exeter	3415	Oxford	2/37	977,734
3706	*John W Wilson*	6/06	Landore	3416	Taunton	5/36	853,782
3707	*Francis Mildmay#*	6/06	Landore	3417	Wellington	4/48	1,142,888

No.	Name	Built	1st depot	1912 No.	Last depot	Withdrawn	Mileage
3708	*Sir Arthur Yorke*	6/06	Cardiff	3418	Southall	8/49	1,309,863
3709		6/06	Landore	3419	Didcot	8/49	1,129.072
3710		6/06	Neyland	3420	Didcot	9/37	924,781
3711		6/06	Neath	3421	Swindon	4/48	1,195,581
3712	*Aberystwyth**	6/06	Cardiff	3422	Severn Tunnel Jcn	3/36	973,138
3713		6/06	Basingstoke	3423	Chester	1/39	968,226
3714		7/06	Landore	3424	Plymouth Laira	5/36	778,728
3715		6/06	Bristol	3425	Swindon	2/38	981,112
3716		7/06	Neyland	3426	Reading	12/49	1,209,310
3717		7/06	Bordesley Jcn	3427	Plymouth Laira	4/38	973,721
3718		7/06	Bordesley Jcn	3428	Worcester	10/36	934,363
3719		7/06	Taunton	3429	Swindon	9/36	870,989
3720	*Inchcape*	8/06	Cardiff	3430	Newton Abbot	12/48	1,121,729
3721		8/06	Bordesley Jcn	3431	Plymouth Laira	12/48	1,181,357
3722		8/06	Cardiff	3432	Hereford	12/49	1,156,178
3723		8/06	Landore	3433	Swindon	4/39	1,030,384
3724	*Joseph Shaw*	8/06	Cardiff	3434	Didcot	7/37	992,975
3725		8/06	Cardiff	3435	Plymouth Laira	11/45	1,155,249
3726		8/06	Cardiff	3436	Gloucester	12/38	1,093,027
3727		9/06	Cardiff	3437	Shrewsbury	3/39	978,636
3728		9/06	Cardiff	3438	Westbury	10/49	1,232,125
3729	*Weston-super-Mare**	9/06	Goodwick	3439	Cardiff	7/36	959,095
3730		9/06	Neath	3440	Worcester	6/48	1,151,755
3731	*Blackbird*	5/09	Tyseley	3441	Plymouth Laira	2/49	1,101,625
3732	*Bullfinch*	5/09	Chester	3442	Shrewsbury	7/48	1,126,708
3733	*Chaffinch*	5/09	Cardiff	3443	Taunton	5/49	1,199,214
3734	*Cormorant*	5/09	Newport	3444	Taunton	6/51	1,153,582
3735	*Flamingo*	5/09	OOC	3445	Gloucester	10/48	997,097
3736	*Goldfinch*	11/09	Neyland	3446	Worcester	12/48	1,084,123
3737	*Jackdaw*	12/09	Hereford	3447	Worcester	4/51	1,006,567
3738	*Kingfisher*	12/09	Basingstoke	3448	Didcot	1/49	1,064,439
3739	*Nightingale*	12/09	Reading	3449	Cheltenham	6/51	1,118,031
3740	*Peacock*	12/09	Stafford Rd	3450	Croes Newydd	12/49	1,008,854
3741	*Pelican*	1/10	Cardiff	3451	Exeter	4/51	1,096,006
3742	*Penguin*	1/10	Bristol	3452	Swindon	4/48	1,064,997
3743	*Seagull*	1/10	Neyland	3453	Reading	11/51	1,070,360
3744	*Skylark*	1/10	Neath	3454	Reading	11/51	1,148,876
3745	*Starling*	1/10	Tyseley	3455	Hereford	6/50	951,641

* name removed as used on later GW locomotives or to avoid passenger confusion

\# 3316 later *Isle of Guernsey*

  3357 also *Royal Sovereign* 1902, *Smeaton* 1903+

  3365 later *Pershore Plum*

  3384 later *Swindon*, then later removed

  3415 later *Stanley Baldwin*

3416 later *Frank Bibby*
3417 later *Charles Grey Mott*
3420 later *Sir Ernest Palmer*
3421 later *David MacIvor*
3423 later *Sir Massey Lopes*
3424 later *Sir N. Kingscote*
3425 later *Sir William Henry*
3704/3414 later *Sir Edward Elgar*
3707/3417 later *Lord Mildmay of Flete*

+ frames combined with parts from 'Duke' 3265 to form prototype of 'Dukedog' but retaining 'Duke' identity, withdrawn from Oswestry depot, 12/49, mileage 1,476,550

3521 class

Dimensions (with '2301' boiler)

Cylinders:	17″ diameter x 24″ stroke
Coupled wheels:	5' 2″ diameter
Bogie wheels:	2' 8″ diameter
Boiler pressure:	150lbpsi (some 160 lbs)
Grate area:	17.2sqft
Heating surface:	1,179sqft (some 1,194.6sqft)
Axle-weight:	14 tons 12cwt maximum
Weight, engine:	41 tons 4cwt
Weight, tender:	34 tons 5cwt
Total weight:	75 tons 5cwt
Tender capacity:	2,500 gallons
Tractive effort (85%):	14,263 lb

Dimensions (with '2301' boiler + Belpaire firebox)

As above, except:

Boiler pressure:	180 lb or 200 lb
Heating surface:	1,193.7sqft
Axle-weight:	14 tons 16cwt maximum
Weight, engine:	41 tons 16cwt
Total weight:	76 tons
Tractive effort (85%):	17,120 lb (at 180lb boiler pressure)

Dimensions (with parallel Standard No.3 coned boiler)

As above, except:

Boiler pressure:	180 lbs
Heating surface:	1,561.65sqft
Grate area:	21.35sqft
Axle-weight:	15 tons 6cwt maximum
Weight, engine:	45 tons
Total weight:	79 tons 5cwt
Tractive effort (85%):	17,120lb

Dimensions (with long tapered boiler)

As above, except:

Boiler pressure:	200lb
Heating surface:	1,425.7sqft
Grate area:	20.35sqft
Axle-weight:	15 tons 18cwt maximum
Weight, engine:	46 tons 3cwt
Total weight:	80 tons 8cwt
Tractive effort (85%):	19,020lb

Weight diagrams

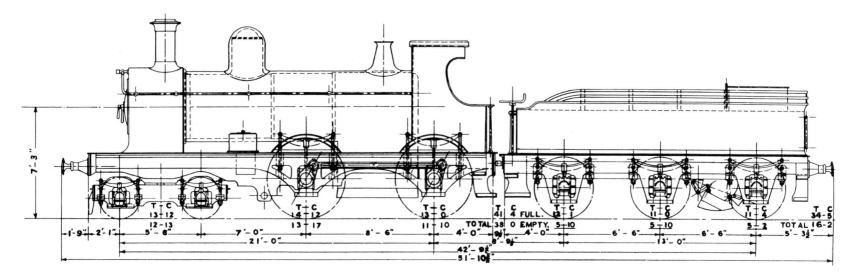

3521 Class as built

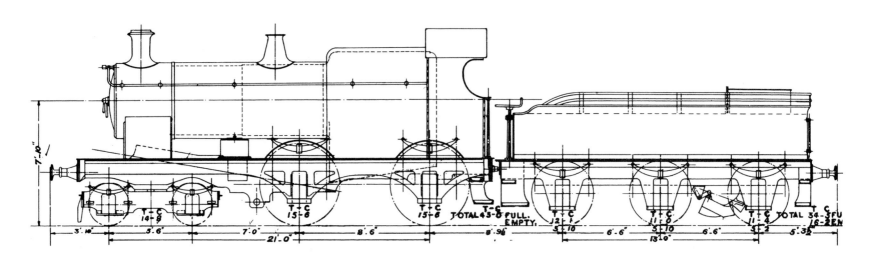

3521 Class - No.3 coned boiler

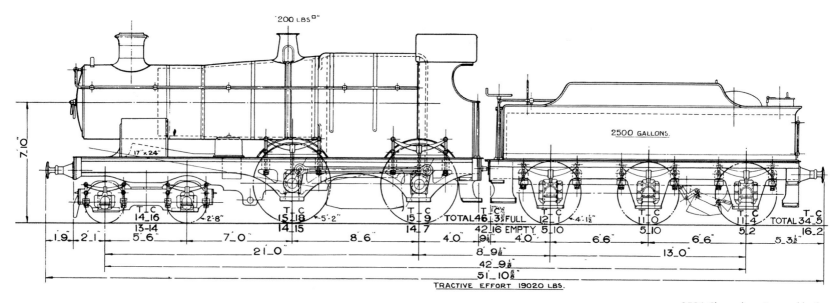

3521 Class - long tapered boiler

Statistics

No.	Built as 0-4-2T	Built as 4-4-0	1st depot	Last depot	Withdrawn	Mileage
3521	1887	8/99	Frome	Machynlleth	10/31	937,467
3522	1887	5/99	Truro	Worcester	1/25	907,569
3523	1887	10/99	Penzance	Cheltenham	5/27	836,938
3524+	1887	3/02	Tondu	Gloucester	10/27	1,099,674
3525+	1887	3/01	Didcot	Gloucester	5/21*	115,278**
3526	1887	6/00	Reading	Evesham	10/27	855,437
3527	1887	2/00	Cardiff	Worcester	4/27	1,015,661
3528+	1887	6/00	Launceston	Reading	7/27	1,081,021
3529	1887	4/00	Salisbury	Kidderminster	4/31	1,092,648
3530	1888	11/99	Plymouth	Carmarthen	3/22	879,289
3531+	1888	6/01	Cardiff	Worcester	11/27	1,047,674
3532+	1888	10/02	Newport	Taunton	3/28	912,510
3533+	1888	6/01	Newport	Worcester	2/29	1,142,620
3534	1888	12/99	Worcester	Carmarthen	10/27	1,024,371
3535	1888	8/99	Plymouth	Kidderminster	12/28	964,078
3536+	1888	10/01	Abergavenny	Gloucester	11/28	1,002,039
3537	1888	5/99	Falmouth	Gloucester	9/28	897,274
3538	1888	10/00	Cardiff	Worcester	7/27	917,387
3539	1888	1/00	Salisbury	Bristol SPM	10/27	940,015
3540+	1888	9/00	Didcot	Gloucester	11/27	1,090,015
3541	1888	10/99	Plymouth	Truro	11/13	approx 626,000
3542	1888	3/99	Truro	Aberystwyth	3/26	No record**
3543	1888	9/99	Plymouth	Winchester	9/28	No record**

No.	Built as 0-4-2T	Built as 4-4-0	1st depot	Last depot	Withdrawn	Mileage
3544	1888	5/00	Didcot	Aberystwyth	2/27	No record**
3545	1888	8/00	Pontypool Rd	Machynlleth	4/31	953,908
3546	1889	1/00	Cardiff	Machynlleth	3/27*	925,781
3547+	1889	1/02	Malvern Wells	Barnstaple	10/27	1,074,741
3548+	1889	3/01	Pembroke Dock	Gloucester	8/29	1,111,367
3549	1889	8/99	Cardiff	Winchester	9/28	929,857
3550	1889	7/00	Trowbridge	Westbury	10/29	949,142
3551+	1889	12/00	Plymouth	Didcot	6/29	1,030,375
3552	1889	10/00	Newport	Bristol Bath Rd	11/29	925,185
3553	1889	1/99	Truro	Bristol Bath Rd	11/28	913,781
3554	1889	2/00	Plymouth	Aberystwyth	6/30	905,940
3555	1889	4/00	Plymouth	Kidderminster	9/29	944,580
3556+	1889	8/01	Birmingham	Cheltenham	10/27	1,132,146
3557	1889	11/99	Stourbridge	Kidderminster	5/34	1,205,448
3558+	1889	12/01	Abergavenny	Evesham	9/27	880,696
3559+	1889	1/01	Plymouth	Worcester	11/28	1,187,527
3560	1891	9/99	Truro	Didcot	10/28	806,663

3521 – 3540 built as standard gauge 0-4-2Ts, rebuilt as 0-4-4Ts between 1890 and 1892. 3541-3559 built as Broad Gauge saddle tank 'convertibles', rebuilt as side tank 0-4-4Ts in 1890-91, and converted to standard gauge in 1892.

  * Sold to Cambrian Railway & returned to GW fleet in 1923

** Further mileage figures lost

  + rebuilt from 0-4-4T with coned boiler

Dukedog class

Dimensions

Cylinders:	18" diameter x 26" stroke
Coupled wheels:	5' 8" diameter
Bogie wheels:	3' 8" diameter (3' 2" for 3265 only)
Boiler pressure:	180lbpsi
Heating Surface:	1,190.2sqft
Grate area:	17sqft
Axle-weight:	15 tons 8cwt
Tender capacity:	3,500 gallons, 6 tons coal
Weight, engine:	49 tons
Weight, tender:	40 tons
Total weight:	89 tons
Tractive effort (85%):	18,955lb

Weight diagrams

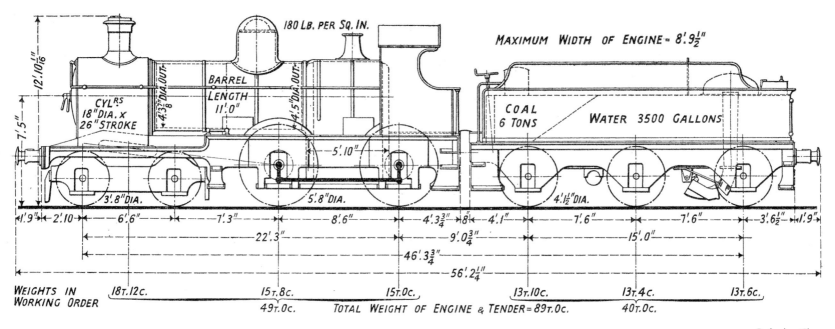

Dukedog Class

Statistics

No.	Name	Built	1st depot	1946 No.	Last depot	Withdrawn	Mileage
3200	*Earl of Mount Edgcumbe*	5/36	Aberystwyth	9000	Machynlleth	3/55	487,182
3201	*St Michael#*	3/36	Oswestry	9001	Oswestry	4/54	482,165
3202	*Earl of Dudley*	6/36	Aberystwyth	9002	Aberystwyth	5/54	425,666
3203	*Earl Cawdor*	7/36	Oswestry	9003	Machynlleth	10/55	573,006
3204	*Earl of Dartmouth*	8/36	Machynlleth	9004	Shrewsbury	7/60	518,121
3205	*Earl of Devon*	9/36	Machynlleth	9005	Oswestry	7/59	506,490
3206	*Earl of Plymouth*	11/36	Didcot	9006	Didcot	9/48	253,823
3207	*Earl of St Germans*	12/36	Tyseley	9007	Tyseley	8/48	211,314
3208	*Earl Bathurst*	2/37	Crewe	9008	Machynlleth	7/57	377,011
3209	*Earl of Radnor*	2/37	Cheltenham	9009	Machynlleth	7/57	376,682
3210	*Earl Cairns*	4/37	Aberystwyth	9010	Oswestry	7/57	327,789
3211	*Earl of Ducie*	3/37	Oswestry	9011	Swindon	7/57	347,297
3212	*Earl of Eldon*	5/37	Shrewsbury	9012	Machynlleth	7/57	403,072
3213	*(Earl of Powis)**	6/37	Aberystwyth	9013	Machynlleth	12/58	448,051
3214	*(Earl Waldegrave)**	8/37	Machynlleth	9014	Croes Newydd	10/60	504,706
3215	*(Earl of Clancarty)**	10/37	Didcot	9015	Machynlleth	6/60	324,000
3216	*(Earl St Aldwyn)**	12/37	Oswestry	9016	Machynlleth	7/57	368,482
3217	*(Earl of Berkeley)**	3/38	Aberystwyth	9017	Machynlleth	10/60**	422,597
3218	*(Earl of Birkenhead)**	4/38	Tyseley	9018	Oswestry	6/60	355,734

No.	Name	Built	1st depot	1946 No.	Last depot	Withdrawn	Mileage
3219	(Earl of Shaftesbury)*	6/38	Gloucester	9019	Tyseley	11/48	258,258
3220		11/38	Oswestry	9020	Machynlleth	7/57	426,490
3221		11/38	Oswestry	9021	Machynlleth	12/58	444,591
3222		12/38	Oswestry	9022	Aberystwyth	8/57	445,798
3223		2/39	Swindon	9023	Swindon	7/57	287,985
3224		2/39	Shrewsbury	9024	Machynlleth	9/57	327,357
3225		4/39	Aberystwyth	9025	Aberystwyth	3/56	379,731
3226		6/39	Oswestry	9026	Oswestry	8/57	392,426
3227		6/39	Aberystwyth	9027	Oswestry	8/57	385,007
3228		12/39	Oswestry	9028	Croes Newydd	9/57	400,335
3265	Tre Pol and Pen	1/30	Didcot	9065	Oswestry	12/49	1,476,550***

* name allocated but not fixed
** preserved on the Bluebell Railway
*** 558,000 approx in 'Dukedog' form
\# renamed Earl of Dunraven, 1937

BIBLIOGRAPHY

CASSERLEY, H.C. & **ASHER** L.L., *Locomotives of British Railways Great Western Group*, Andrew Dakers Ltd, 1958
DRAYTON, John, *Across the Footplate Years*, Ian Allan, 1986
HOLCROFT, H., *Great Western Locomotive Practice 1837-1947*, Locomotive Publishing Company, 1957
NOCK, O.S., *Great Western 4-4-0s Part 1, Inside Cylinder Classes 1894-1910*, David & Charles, 1977
NOCK, O.S., *Great Western 4-4-0s Part 2, 'Counties' to the Close 1904-1961*, David & Charles, 1978
NOCK, O.S., *Fifty Years of Western Express Running*, Edward Everard Ltd, 1954
NOCK, O.S., *Four Thousand Miles on the Footplate*, Ian Allan, 1952
RCTS, *Locomotives of the Great Western Parts 1-7*
ROWLEDGE, J.W.P., *GWR Locomotive Allocations*, David & Charles, 1986
RUSSELL, J.H., *Great Western Engines, A Pictorial Record*, Oxford Publishing Company, 1978

INDEX